RISKY BUSINESS

Church Hiring and Volunteer Selection:

A Legal and Policy Guide

by

Lynn Robert Buzzard

Susan Edwards

Published Jointly by

Church-State Resource Center
Norman A. Wiggins School of Law
Campbell University
Buies Creek, North Carolina

Baptist State Convention of North Carolina
Cary, North Carolina

Published by J.W. Edwards, Inc
Ann Arbor, Michigan. Jointly with
The Church-State Resource Center,
Campbell University and The Baptist State
Convention of North Carolina.

Printed by Edwards Brothers, Inc
Lillington, North Carolina.

ISBN 1-886569-00-2

94 95 96 97 98   5 4 3 2 1

Cover and page C-2, pg 2 artwork by Tonia Dean Michno
Appendix page artwork by Kathy Herring

Authors:

Lynn R. Buzzard

B.A., Duke University
M.A.T., Duke University
M. Div., Duke Divinity School
J.D., DePaul University

Professor of Law
Director, Church-State Resource Center
Norman Adrian Wiggins School of Law
Campbell University

Susan Edwards

B.A., Western Michigan University (Business and Management)
J.D. (1995), Norman Adrian Wiggins School of Law
Research Assistant, Church-State Resource Center

Professional and career focus on
employment law and practices.

Church-State Resource Center

The Center is a division of the Norman Adrian Wiggins School of Law.
Its purpose is to be a resource to attorneys, church leaders and local congregations
in understanding the impact of law on the life of the church and its ministries.
It publishes a variety of resources including the
Minister's Legal Desk Reference: North Carolina Edition,
and the monthly professional legal periodical, *The Religious Freedom Reporter.*

Table of Contents

Two Disclaimers

#1 - Legal Limits of this Guide

While this Guide is intended to provide helpful information to churches on their potential legal risks and means of minimizing legal problems related to hiring, it is important to recognize that there are serious limitations on our ability to provide precise legal guidance. First, laws change and certainly in the employment, discrimination and tort liability arenas, these are rapidly evolving areas of law. Second, the law is very fact-sensitive and thus the generalized rules of law noted here may have a different impact in certain specific factual settings. Third, while we have attempted to be comprehensive and accurate within the limited space and purpose, given courts or administrative agencies may apply or interpret the law differently.

For all these reasons it is important in the context of any specific legal issues or disputes to consult with legal counsel and others familiar with labor law to review the legal questions and choices in the context of the specific situation.

#2 - Limits of Law

There is a danger and a tragedy reflected in this Guide. The tragedy is that far too much of our life in contemporary culture and the church has been consumed with law, legal duties and risks. As the Dean of the Campbell Law School quipped: "We once had a legal system of "fault", then we had "no fault" and now we have "your fault." Everyone is looking for someone to sue. We have become the most litigious society in the world. Blaming and seeking money for "damages" has replaced community, forgiveness, and other qualities essential for common life. The authors take no joy in many of the recommendations made in this Guide. While some of them we believe are fully appropriate to assure church responsibility and effectiveness, we know that many of them are a response to a "legal ambush" waiting to happen.

The danger is that a church, given the legalization of so many relationships in our society, may think that complying with these legal guidelines is somehow the "key" question. Nothing could be further from the truth. Whenever a church lets the law dominate and control its decisions and its witness, it has lost its soul. There may be occasions (perhaps of growing frequency), when churches will have to say "No" to law in order to maintain integrity. That has been the case throughout history from the early church to the faithful church in Soviet Russia or China. Fortunately, still, most of what the law requires, however burdensome and meddlesome, does not yet attack the core witness of the church. But it is important for churches and believers to remember that our charter is not the civil law, not even the Constitution, but the Word of God. Baptists have a long history of honoring that core faithfulness. This Guide, therefore, is certainly not meant in any way to minimize the necessity of the essentially spiritual process which must be at the center of all hiring decisions. The discernment of the gifts of the Spirit to God's people, the sense of calling and vocation, the body of Christ seeking in prayer the leading of the Lord: these are the tasks which must consume the passion of the church. Being conscious of the law and legal risks is secondary to that spiritual process.

Section A: OVERVIEW

1. Introduction

2. Legal Issues

I. THREE MAJOR FACTORS REQUIRING GREAT CARE IN HIRING

II. ADVANTAGES OF A WELL-PLANNED HIRING PROCESS

III. THE UNIQUENESS OF CHURCH WORKERS—AND IMPLICATIONS

IV. CHURCH GOVERNANCE AND PERSONNEL POLICY

This "Guide to Church Hiring" is being jointly produced by the Baptist State Convention of North Carolina and the Church-State Resource Center at Campbell University's School of Law because of increased questions and concerns among churches about hiring practices and policies:

What laws apply to churches when they hire ministers or staff?
Can a church "discriminate" in favor of Baptists?
Is the church liable if it hires a day-care worker who abuses children?
What is the difference between an employee and an independent contractor?
Should the church do criminal background checks on potential employees?
Can a church refuse to hire someone because of his private conduct?*
How can a church find out the real truth about job applicants, even candidates for pastor?

These questions are frequently asked of Convention staff and the Church-State Resource Center. The employer-employee relationship has become much more complex; and churches are concerned not only how to avoid legal pitfalls, but also how to make decisions as responsibly as possible.

I. THREE MAJOR FACTORS REQUIRING GREAT CARE IN HIRING:

Spiritual Integrity

Clearly for churches, the most important mandate for care in hiring is a spiritual concern—a concern to be good stewards of the resources we have for ministry, to equip and enable God's people for the church's ministry, and to utilize the diversity of gifts in the body of Christ.

Effective Management

A second basis for care in hiring is to assure the development of an effective team of personnel—paid and voluntary—who can provide the leadership and skills necessary to achieve the church's objectives. As in the biblical examples of Nehemiah, or the mission work of the early church, the work of God is to be prayerfully and carefully planned and organized to maximize our corporate effectiveness. Sound management is not a substitute for spiritual focus, but it is an expression of our commitment to excellence in all we do.

Compliance with Law

The law increasingly impacts employment practices. While churches are exempt from many regulatory laws, they are not exempt from all; and the trend is toward more regulation and less exceptions. Violations of civil law and substantial tort liability for harms caused by others may result from failures to take reasonable care in hiring. In many cases, even if the law does not require some particular approach or policy by churches, the law may express sound values and principles which the church might voluntarily seek to implement. For example, the law's prohibition against discrimination against the handicapped or aged may not always apply to churches, but certainly most churches would not want to discriminate on these bases and might well consider policies and practices which assure they do not.

---

* Authors today encounter difficult choices with the use of pronouns which reflect gender. We have chosen throughout to use "his" and "he" rather than the more cumbersome, though perhaps more technically correct, "his/her" "he/she." This use is intended, however, to be generic, and not to reflect any suggestion that certain jobs are "male," or to reflect a lack of appreciation for the major role of women in church employment.

II. ADVANTAGES OF A WELL-PLANNED HIRING PROCESS

- **Competence**: Assure that those hired are appropriately gifted and skilled for the ministries they will facilitate, and thus increase effectiveness, better employee retention and performance.

- **Consistency and Faithfulness**: Apply biblical standards and principles in selecting church staff and personnel and assure the integrity of the ministry.

- **Fairness**: Avoid inappropriate favoritism or bias and give an opportunity to persons to explore God's call for them in church work.

- **Protect Others**: Assure that those hired do not create a risk of harm to others by their lack of abilities and training, or by avoidable risks of misconduct such as sexual abuse or dangerous driving.

- **Avoid Unnecessary Lawsuits**: Take steps to minimize liability for negligence in hiring.

III. THE UNIQUENESS OF CHURCH WORKERS—AND IMPLICATIONS

A. The Spiritual and Religious Focus

As we shall see throughout the law, there are statutory and constitutional privileges which may apply because of the very special religious nature of church employment. Most obvious is the legitimacy of the church selecting employees with a view to their spiritual commitments to the ministry. This essentially spiritual and religious process has substantial implications: it certainly heightens the concern to effectively identify those with the requisite gifts and calling, and it makes the legal context more complex because of principles of separation of church and state and the free exercise of religion.

B. The Informal Nature of the Process

Both because of the special spiritual nature of the church and also because it is typically a small, local and closely related fellowship, most employment practices are casual and informal. Persons are often hired without many of the processes typical in business. Jobs may not be advertised, employees may be from the local church, and the documentation is minimal. A personnel committee may be involved, but even their process will emphasize informal means rather than forms and records.

There is much to commend these informal processes, and they are likely to continue to dominate the small church which only employs perhaps a janitor, secretary and pastor. However, these informal approaches can pose some serious problems when difficulties or challenges arise. The lack of records, the lack of careful review of applicants' qualifications, and misunderstandings about expectations may create personnel problems and even serious legal problems. In certain instances, such as employment of day care workers, counselors, and pastors, it is clear that these informal processes are seriously inadequate and that a more structured and planned process is essential.

C. The Predominance of Volunteers Instead of Paid Staff

While most businesses are predominantly staffed by paid employees, churches are the opposite. Most of the work of the church is done by volunteers—Sunday School teachers, youth workers, camp counselors, church picnic organizers, drivers for a youth outing, nursery supervisors, etc.

All these volunteers may, just like employees, represent the church and have serious responsibilities. Such volunteers normally provide enormous beneficial service to the church and its ministry. Of course, sometimes problems arise: a driver's negligence injures the youth, a day-care volunteer may abuse a child, a camp supervisor may not give adequate attention at the camp swimming hole, a youth counselor may get sexually involved with one of the youth, or a cook may inadequately prepare food.

The key here is to recognize that volunteers, as much as employees, need to be carefully chosen to be sure they are spiritually appropriate and have the proper skills and personal qualities to perform the tasks. As we shall see, those who are going to drive the youth to camp should be chosen to assure they are safe drivers, and those who work with children that they do not pose an unreasonable risk to the health and safety of the children.

Because they are volunteers, this sometimes makes it more difficult to exercise review and careful selection. However, especially in areas of high potential risk and great responsibility, such as working with children and driving vehicles, churches need to give more careful attention than simply asking for volunteers at the end of the church service.

D. Frequent Lack of Immediate Supervision and Control

The nature of the work of most church volunteers and even many employees is that the supervision is not only informal; it may almost be non-existent, or certainly episodic. Nursery workers, Sunday School teachers, adults accompanying youth on a trip, and even employees like custodians receive very little training or supervision. In practice, there is little job performance review or accountability. Even the pastor, once hired, is often not subject to careful scrutiny or job assessment. Only when crises arise is there any discussion of such matters as style, use of time, or priorities. This is inevitable in a largely volunteer organization, but may pose serious problems. When there is no meaningful supervision or accountability, employee misconduct—willful or merely negligent—often goes undetected. Rumors of problems may finally arise but be initially dismissed as gossip. A lack of lines of authority may result in confusion about who should act in checking on the performance of volunteers and employees.

Certainly in high-risk areas (such as child-care activities, supervision of dependent persons, or transportation), churches need to take much more seriously staff and volunteer supervision and accountability; but these factors also suggest that because of the large measure of individual responsibility without direct supervision, great care needs to be taken in hiring or securing volunteers initially.

IV. CHURCH GOVERNANCE AND PERSONNEL POLICY

Who's in charge here?

That is a frequent question in churches—sometimes in jest, sometimes seriously. In many churches which emphasize informal structures and close fellowship, the governing structures and assignment of responsibilities are not always clear. Decisions are made consensually and informally. However, in the hiring area, it is perhaps more important than in some other administrative arenas, to develop clear systems for responsibility in hiring, and, of course, beyond that, in such areas as supervision and even dismissal.

Churches should review their Bylaws and other policy provisions and assure that there is an understanding of where the responsibility rests to pursue an effective hiring process. Our recommendation is that churches develop specific written provisions which include two key elements:

1. *Identification of Hiring/Nominating Responsibility*

What church body has responsibility for identification of candidates for positions? Who will be responsible for implementing hiring procedures? What church body has final authority to hire? Also, who trains, supervises and disciplines employees? Who reviews the performance? Who has authority to terminate or recommend termination?

2. *Required Procedures*

The essence of this Guide is that there are certain procedures which churches should follow—varying, of course, with the nature of the job. The local church should adopt some policy about the expected procedures. It need not spell out every single procedural step, but the basic expectations should be clear and contained in some written document or through reference to other documents such as this Guide.

See Appendix for some sample provisions.

For purposes of administrative structure, it may be best to conceive of four types of "employees": senior pastors, other ministerial staff, non-ministerial staff, and volunteers.

A. Senior Pastors

In the context of senior pastor hiring, most Baptist churches have a rather well-defined process involving a Pastor Search Committee presenting a nominee to the whole church in conference for a call. It is this Pastor Search Committee which is likely to bear the primary responsibility for developing a thorough and effective search process, including addressing some of the issues discussed here. See Section IV for a fuller discussion.

After the pastor has been called, the practice of churches is much more mixed in terms of accountability. In some churches, the deacons serve in that capacity with the effectiveness being largely dependent on the styles of both the pastor and deacons. In other churches, a pastoral relations committee may serve some similar functions.

What is clear to many church leaders today is that some systems of pastoral accountability are essential, and that we have too often treated pastors as unaccountable CEO's or lone rangers. The result is not only the embarrassing occasional serious moral lapses, but the more common problems of pastoral isolation or excessive authoritarianism. There is certainly no biblical warrant to separate the pastor from the mutual accountability which is an aspect of Christian community. Churches should consciously develop structures and systems which invite accountability in a spirit of positive encouragement and admonition.

B. Other Ministerial Staff

Beyond the senior pastor, when it comes to employing associate pastors, youth ministers and other ministerial staff, the process varies widely among Baptist churches. Some employ a process similar to the pastor-search process, simply including the senior pastor as an active committee member. Others have a much abbreviated procedure in which the senior pastor basically selects someone and recommends him to the church. In still other churches, the task may be given to a personnel committee.

Regardless of where responsibility is located, that body should take responsibility for addressing the concerns suggested in this Guide.

C. Non-Ministerial Staff

Typically, staff at this level (secretaries, janitors, lawn maintenance) are hired very informally by the church, often with the Pastor playing the primary role, or in more structured situations through a Personnel Committee. In either case, because of the informality of the process, those responsible may tend to short-circuit effective and needed procedures. While such abbreviated processes will usually not result in great harm or liability, the risks are such that we believe they warrant the extra care to assure that the process is sound.

The church should, by internal printed policies, give guidance to a Personnel Committee, or may refer them to other sources such as this Guide. Whatever the form, most such committees are unlikely to have sufficient experience in this area to carry out their responsibilities without some guidance. An experienced administrator should be on the committee or available to them to assist in developing proper procedures.

D. Volunteers

The problems created by volunteers are discussed more thoroughly in Section IV. At this point, it is worth noting that in the case of volunteers, churches traditionally do almost no screening and have no review process. Given the types of activities of volunteers such as supervision of children and youth, driving, operating equipment, food service, etc., this failure to engage in any selectivity may create risks the church has not appreciated. Procedures of selection appropriate to the nature of the duties of the volunteers and the kinds of supervision which will be available are increasingly crucial. See Section IV: Volunteers.

E. Special Programs, e.g., Day Care

Where churches have special highly structured programs such as Day Care, there is more of a tendency to have some structured hiring process, at least with paid employees. The whole child-care arena is discussed at more length in Section IV. At this point, it is simply important to note that the hiring process and identification of responsibility becomes both more crucial and more formal in such situations.

A- 2. Legal Landscape

I. CAN'T ESCAPE THE LAW

II. SOURCES OF LEGAL DUTIES

III. DO THESE LAWS CONTROL CHURCH EMPLOYMENT PRACTICES?

IV. GENERAL OVERVIEW OF EMPLOYMENT LAW AND HIRING RISKS

V. NEGLIGENT HIRING CLAIMS

VI. "DISCRIMINATION" CLAIMS AND CHURCH EMPLOYMENT PRACTICES

VII. FREE EXERCISE OF RELIGION AND HIRING FREEDOMS

I. CAN'T ESCAPE THE LAW

While churches used to rarely need to consult the law books, that is much less true today. Government regulations affect churches in many ways—taxes, property use, building codes, licenses, etc. Besides the statutes, the other unavoidable law is the increasing liability which is imposed on organizations and employers for the acts of their employees, including claims that the employer was negligent in hiring the employee who caused the harm.

A. Employment Law

Employment law is one of the most rapidly growing areas of federal and state regulation. Today, many aspects of employment are regulated by federal, state and even local laws. These cover not only the hiring process, but wage and benefit programs, working conditions, pension programs, unfair labor practices, sexual harassment, age discrimination, discrimination against the "handicapped," and many other areas.

Thus, a consideration of legal and policy questions about "hiring" is only one aspect of a much larger pattern of government regulation of labor law. While churches are exempt from many of these regulations that govern businesses and other employers, they are subject to some of the requirements.

B. Tort Law—Injury to Persons or Property Caused by a Person's Misconduct

Churches may run into legal problems not only because of some statute about employment practices, but also because they may be liable for the harms caused by employees, such as injuries caused by the negligent operation of a motor vehicle or child abuse by nursery or day care workers. Thus, even if there is no statute which requires churches to exercise some care in hiring, the risks of substantial liabilities from employee misconduct should warn churches to be careful.

II. SOURCES OF LEGAL DUTIES

A. Public Law
- Federal statutes, e.g., Civil Rights Acts
- State statutes
- County or city statutes/regulations
- Regulations of administrative agencies which deal with labor law or civil rights
- Court decisions interpreting and applying laws and regulations
- Tort liability for harms caused by conduct that breaches a duty of due care

B. Private Law (Agreements)
- Express contracts between parties which create legal obligations by agreement
- Employee handbooks, policies (These may or may not be viewed by courts as part of the employment contract.)
- Past employment practices (These practices may create reasonable expectations on the part of employees so that they too become part of the contract.)

III. DO THESE LAWS CONTROL CHURCH EMPLOYMENT PRACTICES?

A. Often, NO!

1. Many statutes do not apply to churches:

1) Some statutes contain express <u>exceptions</u> for religious organizations for certain kinds of "discrimination."

2) Some statutes prohibiting discrimination only apply if the employer has a certain number of employees, e.g., 20, and most churches do not cross this threshold.

3) Some federal statues only apply to enterprises involved in interstate commerce, and many local churches may be held not to be involved in interstate commerce.*

   *This is a very flexible and uncertain standard with courts and regulators taking sometimes conflicting views. Certainly, large church denominational offices are more likely to be held to be in interstate commerce than are local churches, but a local church with a national television or literature ministry may well be viewed by some as crossing the threshold.

4) Courts may conclude that some statutes, even if they do not provide an exception by the terms of the statute, were not intended by Congress to apply to churches.

2. Constitutional Exceptions

Even if the statutes appear to apply, there MAY be constitutional protections such as the Free Exercise Clause of the First Amendment of the U.S. Constitution, recently reinforced by the Religious Freedom Restoration Act. State constitutions may also provide exceptions.

3. Few Challenges in Practice

As a matter of actual experience, few local churches find their employment practices challenged either by employees or by rejected applicants. Therefore, there is relatively little case law on how courts or agencies would deal with local church issues.

B. However, there are legal implications from hiring practices:

- *Legal Duties*: Some state and federal statutes do impose duties on employers and their hiring practices, and a failure to comply with these duties could produce fines and/or requirements to compensate persons protected by these laws.

- *Liability for Acts of Employees*: Churches are frequently liable for harms and injuries suffered by others because of the negligence of their employees or even volunteers, and thus the church should exercise care in selecting employees and recruiting volunteers.
- *Negligent Hiring Liability*: Churches that do not carefully screen employees who are in especially sensitive positions such as child care, may be liable under a

concept of *negligent hiring* if the employee or volunteer injures others. (See discussion later.)

- *Trend toward Legal Duties*: The trend is toward more regulation and fewer exceptions, so that churches may well need to be aware of the larger legal landscape and expect challengers, probably sooner rather than later.

- *Lawsuit Vulnerability*: Applicants and employees are much more aware these days of their "rights" and willing to use the law to force compliance or obtain compensation for grievances. The day when churches were legally and practically immune from lawsuits is gone.

IV. GENERAL OVERVIEW OF EMPLOYMENT LAW AND HIRING RISKS

To understand the recommendations contained in this Guide, it is essential to understand the legal risks that we are seeking to avoid or minimize. Therefore, an overview of these risks in the employment, and especially, hiring, context will help a church make informed decisions.

A. Employment Law in General

As we have noted, hiring issues are only a part of the much larger employment or labor law arena. This is an area so filled with laws, regulations, contracts, and tort law that it is far beyond our scope here. It is helpful, however, to realize that in the employment area most legal risks, lawsuits or legal duties arise AFTER the hiring process. After an employee is hired, there are several types of legal risks that arise for the employer.

1. Failure to comply with statutes and regulations creates a potential liability both for the employer and can also involve civil penalties

    Tax laws
    Benefit program regulations
    Reporting
    Unsafe work environment
    Discrimination in advancement
    Age discrimination in termination or promotion
    Sexual harassment

2. Liability to the <u>employee</u> for breach of contract by the employer

    For example, failure to provide the benefits, conditions, wages, or whatever of the contract, or to follow the grievance procedures of the contract

3. Liability to <u>others</u> because of acts of the employee during the course of his employment

    Employers are liable for the negligence of employees while they are performing their job. This is called *respondeat superior*—the concept being that the Master (employer) is liable for the acts of the Servant (employee) while the Servant is working for the Master. This arises in many situations, such as when an employee (or volunteer) is driving a vehicle negligently, or leaves a slippery condition on the floor. The employer is not directly responsible, but <u>indirectly</u>. The potential for this kind of liability is a major reason for care in hiring, since a careless employee may create major liability for the employer.

4. Employer liability for harm to <u>others</u> because of the employer's own negligence in training or supervision, or retention of an employee after the employer knew of the risks the employee posed to others

    Here it is not the negligence of the employee that creates the liability, but the negligence of the employer who failed to exercise reasonable care. For example, if a nursery worker injures a child, the plaintiff may claim that the church inadequately trained the person for that task, or was negligent in failing to supervise the work. If the person had a history of carelessness, perhaps a plaintiff may claim the church was negligent in not removing the person from that responsibility.

Notice—these liabilities all arise AFTER a person has been employed. They are, therefore, not the specific focus of this HIRING guide.

B. Liabilities Directly Related to Hiring Process

There are specific liabilities which arise that are directly linked to what goes on, or doesn't go on, in the hiring process itself. To oversimplify a bit, we might recognize three types:

1. Liabilities based on claims by those <u>not</u> hired

    This would arise where someone claimed the church had violated some federal or state statute that barred some discrimination—and the claimant seeks financial recovery for being denied a position, or the opportunity to fairly compete for it. (Discussed more fully below and throughout this Guide.)

2. Claims of an <u>employee</u> asserting that the job was not what was offered and accepted

    This type of claim relates to the job description, interview, and offer—and the claim is that some aspect of the job is different than offered. It is in many respects a "contract" type claim—a breach of a promise. Perhaps the benefits are not as represented, or the job required some skill, e.g., computer literacy, that was not mentioned, or required evening work which was not mentioned.

3. Claims of <u>other</u> persons who have been injured by the employee, alleging the employer was negligent in hiring the person because the employer knew, or should have known, that that person posed an unreasonable risk of harm to others. This is a claim for **negligent hiring,** discussed more fully in the next section.

Summary of Types of
LIABILITIES

Hiring Phase	Post-Hiring Phase
Liability to state and rejected employee for violation of law in hiring process, e.g., discrimination—based on statutes	Liability to employee for post-hiring discrimination or other wrong, e.g., impermissible discrimination in promotion, benefits or termination, sexual harassment, unsafe environment, etc.
Liability to hired person for breach of contract job is not as described during course of employment	Liability to others for the negligence because of employee who injured another
Liability to injured third persons because of employer's own negligence in hiring the person who caused the injury	Liability to others because employer was negligent in failing to reasonably train, supervise or otherwise prevent employee's harm

V. NEGLIGENT HIRING CLAIMS

A. Illustrations

Negligent hiring is a growing type of claim, especially in certain specific contexts such as child care, and even has been asserted in the hiring of ministers. For example, a church hires a day-care worker and fails to make any inquiry into his background. After a child is abused, it is discovered that a routine inquiry into references or criminal background would have revealed several incidents of alleged child abuse by the employee prior to his employment. Or suppose a pastor is hired by a church and then sexually abuses a child. A background check would have revealed a pattern of brief pastorates with evasive recommendations from other churches, but the church did no follow up at all. Or consider a youth counselor who is employed and then takes sexual liberties with young girl campers. The church hired the youth counselor from a local college, but did not obtain references, call any previous employers, nor ask about prior experience. These steps would have revealed that he had been accused of such acts at a previous summer camp and had been removed from his position.

In all these instances, the injured person will likely claim that the church was negligent in hiring the person—as well, perhaps, as claiming negligence in supervision, etc.

B. Wide Scope of Liability in Negligent Hiring Claims

It is critical to note that in this latter, "negligent hiring" claim, the liability is much more extensive than the _respondeat superior_ liability for the negligence of an employee. Under _respondeat superior_, the employer is ONLY liable for acts which were in furtherance of the interests of the employer—part of the job. Normally, acts of a personal nature and willful criminal acts or intentional harms to another are not imputed to the employer. However, in a negligent hiring claim, almost any act of the employee that occurs during working time, or is in some way connected with the job or work place, or which harms persons where the relationship was derived from the employment may create liability. For example, if a night security guard at a facility robs or rapes an employee or customer who was leaving the facility (or even finds out who they are and later attacks them in their home), the employer is probably NOT liable under _respondeat superior_ because the criminal acts were not part of his employment. However, if the security guard were hired without reasonable inquiries into his appropriateness for the job, and if such inquiries would have placed the employer on warning of the employee's dangerous tendencies, then the employer might well be liable. Again, it is not because of the watchman's wrong-doing alone, but because the employer was wrong (negligent) in hiring a person for that kind of a job without appropriate inquiries into his fitness for the job.

C. The Reasonableness TEST

1. Elements in a Negligence Claim

In any "negligence" action such as negligent hiring, the key is whether the person acted reasonably. An employer is not liable merely because someone is injured. The employer is not like an insurer who must pay no matter what. Under a negligent hiring theory, there is no liability UNLESS several elements can be shown:

    1) There must be an injury, and
    2) The injury must be caused by the defendant's conduct (or lack of action)
    3) The defendant must have been negligent—that is, his action (or lack thereof) was a breach of some duty (such as a failure to take reasonable measures to protect against the risks which created the injury.)

2. What is Reasonable?

What is reasonable is a somewhat elusive standard, and in any legal claim, may end up being decided by a jury. The law says what is reasonable is what an ordinarily prudent person in similar circumstances would do. For example, a reasonable person exercising care would not leave a slippery substance on a walkway without a warning, or leave an unbarricaded large hole in the ground in an area where children played, or have a high deck without a railing.

3. Reasonableness DEPENDS on the CIRCUMSTANCES.

Examples:

If a church is hiring a day-care worker, what is reasonable will be quite different from what is reasonable if it is hiring someone to mow the lawn. In one case, reasonableness is likely to require much more inquiry into background, personal traits, training, experience, any association with misconduct toward children, education, etc.

Reasonable selection of volunteers to build a habitat home in the community will be quite different from volunteers to live with junior high kids at camp for a week. In the latter case, reasonableness would include questions of maturity, prior misconduct, life-style habits, first aid abilities, and perhaps driving record. The home builder, however, might raise questions about technical skills and experience so he doesn't pose an unreasonable risk to himself or others.

"Circumstances" in negligent hiring cases include at least the following: the nature of the task, the risks created by the activities/tasks of the employee, the degree of responsibility and autonomy being given the employee, and the nature of the supervision which will be provided.

4. The Circumstances Include What You Know, and _Should_ Know.

Reasonableness not only will include what one does initially in any inquiries or procedures, but how one responds to information obtained. A reference for a pastor which seems not to say much, or is evasive about the reasons the pastor left the last church raises different "reasonable" responses than a similar reference letter for the gardener.

In one case, a court held that a day care which employed a worker without inquiry into whether the worker had been abused as a child was liable for negligent hiring because such persons have a much higher incidence of becoming victimizers themselves. Therefore, the court reasoned, they should have inquired about whether the job applicants had been victims themselves. Hiring without inquiring was negligent.

More elusive is the "should have known" factor. The theory is that if there are things you actually didn't know, but should have known—things a reasonable person would have known from the circumstances and other facts or from a reasonable inquiry—you will be held liable just as if you had known them. This is obviously a bit loose.

5. Unreasonableness May be Shown by Failure to Comply with the Law

There are some things which, for the safety of others, the law requires. Building codes require certain types of exits and lighting. Municipal codes may require fences around home swimming pools. Similarly, states such as North Carolina require certain background checks for day-care workers. Whenever a statutory duty is breached, that is usually sufficient to show that the person did not act reasonably—therefore, was negligent.

D. Playing It Safe

1. Making a Record to Show your Reasonableness

Of course, proving that one acted reasonably is another matter, and to establish that reasonable steps were taken, it is important that records be maintained of what was done—such as reference letters received, inquiries made, and responses, etc. (More on this later.)

2. Go the Second Mile

Since reasonableness can be a bit elastic and depends so much on judgments made after the fact, most employers prefer not to crowd the line too closely. It is safer to be a little extra vigilant and careful, than to later get in an argument in court about whether a given course of action should or should not have been pursued. If there are doubts, check it out!

VI. "DISCRIMINATION" CLAIMS AND CHURCH EMPLOYMENT PRACTICES

A. General Right of Employers to Choose Their Employees

For most of our history, there were virtually no restrictions on whom an employer could choose to hire. The employer could prefer blondes, or Yankees, or people with black suits. The employer was equally free to discriminate against certain persons or groups. The Constitutional requirements of "equal protection" never applied to private employers. Still today, an employer may prefer certain employees or discriminate against certain types of persons UNLESS there is some specific statute which prohibits the discrimination. Thus, for example, since there is no statute prohibiting discriminating against persons who prefer pepperoni pizza, an employer could in most cases hire only pepperoni lovers.

B. Emergence of Limits on Employer Hiring Freedom

We are now accustomed to substantial restrictions on the freedom of employers in their hiring practices. Federal and state statutes now impose on many employers duties not to discriminate on a variety of bases: race, ethnic origin, religion, national origin, gender, age, disabilities, etc. Since you have freedom UNLESS a specific statute limits that freedom, it becomes very crucial to determine whether there is a statute dealing with some preference you wish to exercise, and if there is, whether that statute applies to you.

C. Broad Reach of Discrimination Restrictions

It is important to note that when a statute does prohibit some kind of discrimination, it typically covers a broad range of employment practices including not only initial hiring, but promotions, benefits, terminations, etc.

Further, the prohibited discrimination may be found not only in obvious direct instances such as where an employer refuses to hire, for example, a minority applicant, or a woman, or handicapped person—but also may be found indirectly by the way the employer seeks applicants, describes jobs, asks questions, etc. Civil rights and labor practice agencies not only look at discriminatory purposes, but discriminatory effects. Thus, employers subject to these laws have found themselves liable even without any intentional discrimination when their employment procedures resulted, in effect, in discouraging some protected group. Thus, one must have not only a pure heart, but a pure process.

D. Do These Civil Rights Discrimination Statutes Apply to Churches?

1. Some clearly do not apply .

2. Some provide limited exceptions for churches.

The Civil Rights Act, for example, provides a specific exemption for religious organizations which exempts them from the prohibition on religious discrimination, but does not exempt them from racial discrimination prohibitions.

3. Some do not provide an express exception, but churches would normally not be covered because they do not meet the minimum workforce standards.

As noted above, some statutes have a "trigger" of a certain number of employees before the employer is covered. Most churches usually do not have the requisite number.

4. BUT—it is a very uncertain and evolving area.

Civil rights statutes prohibiting certain kinds of discrimination in employment are relatively recent, and some of the recent statutes such as those dealing with disabled persons are so recent that it remains rather unclear how they will be applied by agencies which are empowered to investigate claims and by courts which must interpret the statutes.

In addition to the problems created by the newness of these statutes, further uncertainty is created for churches by what appears to be inconsistent decisions by courts and agencies as to whether these statutes apply to churches or religious organizations.

In addition to uncertainty about these existing statutes, there is a significant trend toward legislation in these areas; so there are frequently new federal, state or local laws. Thus, a church might be presently exempt from some federal statute, but a state statute basically covering the same area may not exempt churches.

E. Some PRESENT Generalizations About Church Hiring Freedoms

(We will have occasion to discuss many of these in more detail in subsequent sections.)

1. Churches clearly MAY prefer or require all their employees to affirm the doctrine/faith of the employing church—even if the task they perform is not directly religious in character. This freedom would extend to a requirement of membership in a specific denomination or even a specific church.

2. Churches clearly MAY employ virtually any criteria or preference in the employment decisions regarding the clergy—probably NO statutes on discrimination will be applied to restrict clergy employment decisions.

3. Churches PROBABLY may require employees to adhere to standards of behavior, both on and off the job, where those standards are clearly an aspect of the church's religious doctrines and beliefs.

4. Churches PROBABLY may discriminate on the basis of criteria such as gender or marital status, even if statutes generally prohibit such, so long as the gender or marital status preference is clearly one required by the church's doctrine; but absent such doctrinal basis, the church may be subject to any statutory prohibitions.

5. Church employment decisions in hiring for day-care programs, or schools, will probably find their freedom more limited by statutory retractions; but if the programs were genuinely religious in character they would certainly retain the right to prefer or require doctrinal/belief compatibility. It is less clear that they would be exempt from restrictions on age, gender or disability legislation.

6. Church-owned enterprises which are not essentially religious in character, but rather commercial in character, are not normally provided, either by statute or judicial decision, the exemptions provided churches.

7. Any employer may always require an employee to have the skills necessary to perform the job. If a condition of employment is a "bona fide occupation qualification," (BFOQ), then it is always legitimate. Thus, it would be permissible to require that a professor in a college have an earned graduate degree, even if that requirement eliminated many minority candidates.

8. Churches are probably not exempt from statutes which do by their terms include churches, and which deal with prohibited discrimination that does not seem to raise a theological question. Thus, a statute which prohibits discrimination against persons with handicaps, and which by its terms does not exempt churches, would impose its duties on churches as much as other employers.

VII. FREE EXERCISE OF RELIGION AND HIRING FREEDOMS

A. Important Basis For Church Autonomy

The "free exercise of religion" is a constitutional guarantee in the First Amendment. This guarantee has been historically interpreted by the Supreme Court as encompassing broad limits on judicial intrusion into matters of theology and church governance. A principle of "autonomy" has developed from the First Amendment that provides substantial freedoms to churches to establish their own means of discipline, theology, and polity without judicial review. Thus, courts defer to church polity in determining the proper authorities in a church. For example, in Baptist churches governed by congregational polity, courts will not substitute their opinions about the church's course or leadership for the decisions made by the majority acting in proper session.

The principles of free exercise certainly have had an impact on labor law as it relates to churches and religious organizations in at least two ways already briefly noted:

1. Legislatively: Sometimes this free exercise commitment has caused legislators to include specific language providing exceptions to otherwise applicable duties. Religious organizations, for example, are specifically exempt from the prohibition against religious discrimination.

2. Judicially: Even where there is no language in a statute or regulation providing an exemption, the courts may hold that the law cannot be applied in a particular instance because it would be impermissibly intrusive into protected religious exercise. Thus, for example, courts have held that the age discrimination prohibition contained in a federal statute cannot be invoked by clergy to challenge a denomination's retirement policy.

Because of the historic commitments to freedom of religion, and the protections often afforded, many erroneously think that these freedoms make churches nearly immune from the law. Such, however, is not the case, and in fact the protections seem to be diminishing.

B. Judicial Protections of Free Exercise

1. Period of Heightened Protections

Since the early 1960's, the courts had applied a rather protective standard in free exercise cases. The United States Supreme Court had developed an analytical process in free exercise cases which declared that whenever government imposed a burden on a sincerely held religious belief, the government action violated the free exercise clause unless the government could establish two things: first, that the burden was justified by a compelling government interest that overrode the religious rights; and, second, that the means chosen were narrowly tailored to achieve the interest without unnecessarily burdening the rights of religious exercise—a "least intrusive means" requirement.

2. Erosion of Protections

In fact, however, during the 70's and 80's, there was a substantial erosion of the protections of the free exercise of religion. The rigorous test was applied in principle, but, in fact, free exercise claims usually lost. Many courts declined to provide constitutionally based exceptions from general regulations. The courts usually justified this denial either by saying that the regulation did not impose a substantial burden on the free exercise of religion, or by finding a "compelling" government interest that overrode the imposition on religion. Further, courts rarely engaged in any serious review of the "means" to assure they were least intrusive.

3. Near Abolition of Protections

In 1991, this protection was further eroded by the Supreme Court in <u>Employment Division v. Smith</u> which held that the free exercise clause did not provide any protection for religious exercise when the statute was one of general applicability which did not target religion. The effect was that it was no longer necessary for the government to show a compelling interest in order to justify the imposition of a burden on the exercise of religion, nor need the government show that the means it employed were least restrictive. Under this ruling, unless the statute provided some exemption for religious belief, it was almost impossible to successfully argue a constitutionally-grounded exemption from some regulatory scheme including labor law regulations.

4. Religious Freedom Restoration Act

So radical was the Court's decision in <u>Smith</u> that Congress in 1993 adopted the Religious Freedom Restoration Act which restored the pre-<u>Smith</u> requirement that whenever government burdens a sincerely held religious belief, it must demonstrate that that burden is required by a compelling government interest and that the burden is the least intrusive means to achieve the overriding interest.

5. Where do we stand now?

How effective this Act will be in protecting religious freedom is as yet unclear. It is hoped that it will restore sensitivity to religious rights and provide a check on intrusive government. But this may be wishful thinking. What is clear, however, is that the theory of free exercise protection may well fail because courts, unwittingly applying secularist values and notions, are likely to easily find compelling government interests that justify the intrusions into religious liberty. Thus, if the public perception, or even judicial perception, is that some value—e.g., prohibition of sex discrimination or sexual preference discrimination—is a "compelling" interest that is more important than religious freedom rights, then the free exercise clause will not help. It is a very subjective, culturally-conditioned process that often pays more attention to contemporary political values than to long standing religious beliefs and practices.

The bottom line is that the sweep of constitutional protections of church preferences is gradually being reduced, even though in certain areas such as the internal affairs of churches, especially those involving clergy, there remains at present little governmental intrusion.

This Guide suggests ways in which the church may respond to these legal and policy concerns. It is not intended to be exhaustive, and special situations may arise where the church needs to obtain more specific counsel and direction from other church leaders or from legal counsel.

The remainder of this Guide is organized into three sections:

Section B: Hiring Steps: A Recommended Process

Section C: Special Hiring Contexts
    A. Clergy
    B. Child Care and Dependent Persons Care
    C. Volunteers
    D. A Note on Independent Contractors

Section D: Federal Statutory Overview

Appendix
    Forms
    Sample By-Law Provisions
    Bibliography

Section B: Hiring Steps: A Recommended Process

Step # 1. PREPARING A JOB DESCRIPTION

Step # 2. IMPLEMENTING A RECRUITING PROCESS

Step # 3. CREATING AN EMPLOYMENT APPLICATION

Step # 4. OBTAINING SIGNED RELEASE FORMS

Step # 5. UTILIZING APPROPRIATE TESTING

Step # 6. CONDUCTING INTERVIEWS

Step # 7. CHECKING REFERENCES

Step # 8. CHECKING CRIMINAL, FINANCIAL AND DRIVER'S RECORDS

Step # 9. FINAL HIRING AND REJECTIONS

Step # 10. WRAPPING THINGS UP

POSTSCRIPT: ASSURING CONSISTENT PROCESS

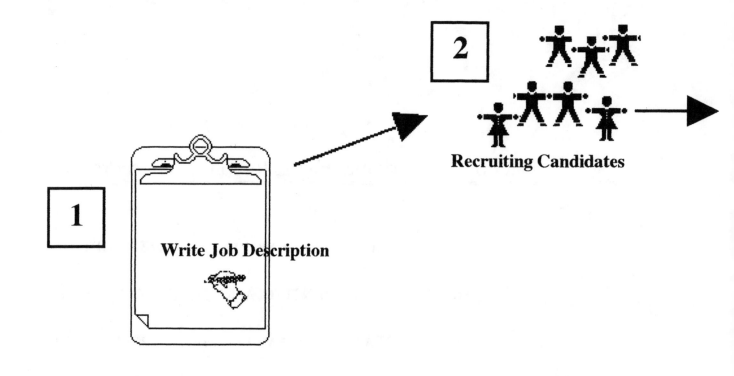

2

Recruiting Candidates

1

Write Job Description

Ten Hiring Steps

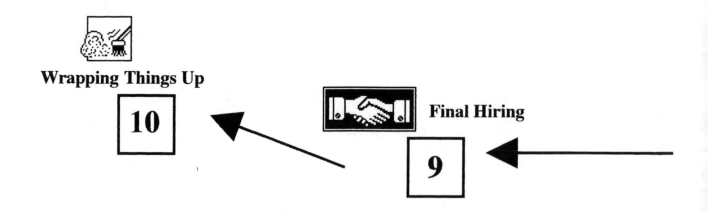

Wrapping Things Up

10

Final Hiring

9

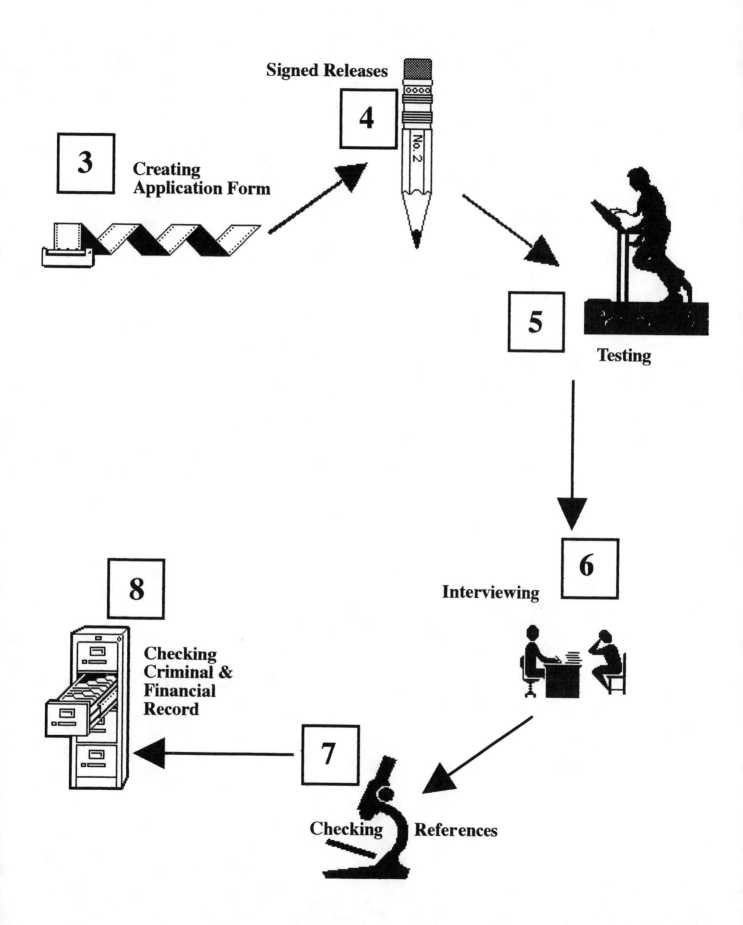

Signed Releases

3 Creating Application Form

4

5 Testing

6 Interviewing

8 Checking Criminal & Financial Record

7 Checking References

Hiring Steps — Preliminary Notes

The following ten steps or stages of a recommended hiring process are not expressly required by any law, and are certainly not magic. They are, however, intended to encourage a thorough process which assures not only that legal risks are minimized, but that a church may have the best opportunity to secure highly qualified and motivated staff to assist in the ministry of the church.

These steps certainly reflect more deliberation and "process" than most churches have traditionally employed. They also reflect a recognition of the different circumstances in which churches find themselves today—greater legal liabilities, more diverse use of employees and volunteers, and less familiarity with potential employees.

Necessity of Adapting These Suggestions

The specific recommendations for each stage will often require some adaptation based on the specific situation of any church: the employees being sought, the nature of the task, whether the church is covered by certain statutes, etc. We have deliberately recommended a comprehensive approach involving rather deliberate processes of evaluation. We have consciously errored in favor of caution and thoroughness.

Is this overkill?

We recognize that for many churches, some of these recommendations which deliberately seek to avoid potential liability from discrimination suits and negligent hiring claims will seem onerous and legally unnecessary because the church may not be subject to many of the discrimination prohibitions. However, even where churches are not bound by legal duties of nondiscrimination, there are good reasons to develop hiring processes which are sensitive to these issues:

1. Churches may choose as a matter of internal policy to seek to avoid any appearance of discrimination.

2. Many churches will believe that many of the concerns the law reflects are legitimate, and that biblical principles would encourage sensitivity to matters like racial or age discrimination.

3. In any event, all churches are subject to potential liabilities from negligent hiring and certainly would want to assure a process that would identify the best employee.

STEP #1: PREPARING A JOB DESCRIPTION

*"If you don't know where you want to go,
any road will get you there"*

Summary Step # 1

Take sufficient time to develop a precise job description that identifies the nature of the tasks to be performed and the required skills and qualities expected. This should also include any special requirements in regard to faith or conduct of employees. This will best assure an efficient and effective process of attracting the best candidates, and will also minimize legal risks created by misunderstandings or surprises after hiring.

The first step is to have a clear sense of the task of the employee or volunteer. What do you want to achieve? What skills and abilities will be required? What are you looking for?

The job description and related documents (such as Statement of Faith, Statement of Moral Obligation, and statement of Church Rules and Policies) are the first documents the church should prepare. These documents present the church's requirements in a uniform manner and quickly establish the criteria on which it will base its hiring decision.

I. WHY IS A JOB DESCRIPTION SO VALUABLE?

- *Requires Church Planning*: The job description should reflect careful church assessment of its needs and requirements rather than general "we need help" thinking.

- *Makes Expectations Clear*: Many problems with employees and frustrations in churches are due to the failure to clearly define tasks and expectations. This results in misunderstandings, conflicting expectations, job dissatisfaction, and poor performance.

- *Encourages Qualified Applicants*: A well-conceived job description may not only avoid problems, it can encourage and even excite qualified applicants. It helps people fit their talents and gifts with opportunities for service and ministry.

- *Guides Selection Among Candidates*: A clear job description can help those who select employees to choose among candidates. It helps avoid employing people merely because they are nice, or church members, or need a job. Instead, the focus can be on how each candidate can fulfill the church's needs.

- *Provides Basis for Accountability*: The job description also provides the basis for reviewing job performance, including areas of skills development or staff support.

- *Legal Protection*: The job description may provide a clear basis for preferring certain candidates over others based on legitimate qualifications for the specific job. (More on this later.)

Creating an accurate and informative job description is vital. Even though it may be a difficult, time-consuming process, it is worth every bit of energy committed to it. Creating a good job description will force the employer to identify exactly what skills and characteristics are required, as well as set an appropriate wage range. Selecting the right person for the job offers great benefits for the church. When the "fit" is right, both the employer and the employee are more likely to be happy, resulting in increased employee retention. Retention is a great cost saver in personnel time, advertising and recruiting costs, and re-training time and costs. Obviously, the right person can also make significant contributions to the church's ministries and services, and can create a positive image for both church members and the secular world.

II. CREATING THE "JOB DESCRIPTION"

A Group Process

Identifying the necessary skills should involve all personnel familiar with the position as well as those who will be working with the new employee. In fact, the best input can be derived from the employee who is vacating the position. The job description should lead a narrowly defined search for the right person and help quickly weed out unsuitable applicants. To create the job description, it is easiest to begin by defining the "skills and characteristics" necessary to the position.

The following questions should be helpful in pinpointing the major skills and characteristics required in the position: (Do not include occasional duties of the position, since these duties may need to be adjusted to accommodate a disabled person who can otherwise perform all of the core functions of the position.)

A. *What are the major job functions, and what percentage of an employee's time will be spent on them?* For example:

- typing, filing
- computer work
- organizing, administering, coordinating
- travel
- phone work (You may need someone with good verbal skills.)
- manual labor or lifting requirements
- interaction with people
(This is very important, since some people prefer NOT to interact with others, but to simply perform their task--a good fit for a production-oriented job like filing, heavy typing, maintenance work, etc.)

Example: A very outgoing person would be well suited to receptionist position, but would probably not be content as a file clerk working alone. Conversely, a reserved person may make an excellent "behind the scenes" worker, but not be happy as a receptionist.

B. Is there teamwork involved with the position, or does the employee work alone?

- consider the strengths and weaknesses of present employees if they will constitute a "team".

C. Is there supervision available? Consider:

- the ability to self-direct may be essential.
- the employee's confidence in his ability to perform the job functions and efficiently work through problems alone may be important.
- training time may be minimal and little supervision may be available, so closely examine applicant's skill level.
- consider that if heavy supervision is available a very independent employee may be stifled in the position.
- what type of applicant will work well with the supervisor's style?

D. How would other employees who will work with this new person describe a "perfect employee"?

E. What skills could be added to this position to increase the productivity or effectiveness of a group, where appropriate?

Consider the following:

- Adding new qualifications could make the position more effective by allowing that person to "swing" to cover other positions, or to eliminate weak links caused by a present employee's weaknesses.

- How important would this new function/ability be in performing the job function? (if not very important, you may not discriminate based solely upon it.)

F. Are there new skills that now need to be utilized, such as computer skills, use of computer networks, etc.?

G. What personal and spiritual qualities are essential for this position (or perhaps any position in the church)?

Putting It All Together

Once responses have been received from others in the organization, preferably by interviewing them in person, examine them closely. This is the time to re-evaluate the job description and adjust what will be required of the new employee's skills. The appropriate body should at this point be able to put together a final job description.

Once a job description is proposed, it should be reviewed through another "lens," the legal lens, and elaborated on where necessary to completely define the required characteristics and skills.

III. MAY THE JOB DESCRIPTION INCLUDE REQUIREMENTS REGARDING RELIGIOUS FAITH, MORAL CONDUCT OR CHURCH RELATIONSHIPS?

Yes!

Some churches have erroneously believed that civil rights laws prohibit them from religious discrimination in hiring church day-care staff, secretaries or other church employees. Some think you can only discriminate where the job itself has a religious component like a minister, counselor or teacher. This is not true.

In almost all situations, churches ARE permitted to "discriminate" based on religious faith and adherence to the moral and doctrinal teachings of the church-employer. While secular employers may not usually discriminate on the basis of religion, an exception exists for churches and certain other religious bodies—an exception often by statute, or if not, then probably by constitutional protections of the free exercise of religion, and the Religious Freedom Restoration Act.

These exceptions exist for two principal reasons: First, there is a legitimate interest in the religious community that those who serve in it share its basic beliefs and affirm and promote them. Any other view would require a church to hire those who would be subversive of its core beliefs. Second, most laws recognize the first amendment's prohibition on intrusion into the internal life of churches and the value of a separation of civil authority from the spiritual and governance aspects of any religious community.

A. Faith Requirements

The right of churches to prefer or require employees to share the faith of the church covers all employees and not just those who may be involved in directly religious or spiritual activities. Thus, it includes the janitor and nursery staff just as much as the pastor or marriage counselor. Of course, churches do not HAVE to impose these requirements, and some would not apply them to jobs like janitor; but almost all would to positions like church secretary and choir director.

If the church has such requirements, they should be clearly set forth in the Job Description for at least three reasons:

1. It will avoid processing applicants who do not meet these expectations, and thus save time for the church and potential applicants.

2. As a matter of fairness, any such expectations should be clearly stated so that they do not come as a surprise to someone who is hired.

3. It establishes both a legal and contractual basis for the dismissal of any employee who fails to conform to these expectations.

Therefore, the church should ask itself these questions as part of preparing the Job Description:

- Does the church have a policy of hiring only those of a particular religious faith or denomination?

- Will the person employed be expected to join the church?

- Are there requirements or expectations of participation in church activities, e.g., regularly attending services? all services? business meetings?

- Is there a moral standard (sometimes referred to as a "role model" rule) necessary to the position?

- Are there applicable Church Rules and Policies about faith or conduct, on or off the job, that the prospective employee should be willing to agree to at the onset?

- Can the church clearly identify the doctrinal, theological basis for its specific conduct requirements? Are these expectations for adherents of this community set forth in writing?

The Job Description may include expectations of conduct and requirements of religious faith, and it should be sufficiently specific to avoid confusion or misunderstanding. It should not say the person must be a "Christian" if it really means a "Baptist." Some of the expectations may be stated by referencing some other document and having that document available. For example, if there is a required Statement of Faith, the church might refer to "The Baptist Faith and Message" as the governing Statement of Faith.

Any "Statement of Faith" should be written and routinely reviewed with all job applicants. It is also extremely important that the policy be consistently applied. Consistent practice will dispel any question of the church's arbitrary application of its policy or its engagement in random discriminatory practices cloaked by a "faith" requirement.

B. Moral Conduct Requirements (Lifestyle/Role Model)

Some positions within religious organizations may require that employees maintain a certain "moral standard," or to position themselves as "role models." Although the secular world generally may not dictate the moral conduct of its employees, a church usually can. If these requirements are dictated by the tenets of the religion, hiring and firing employees based on these standards will most likely be upheld in court.

Again, if this is an anticipated requirement, create a system ahead of time to outline the requirement, define its importance, explain upon which religious tenet it is based, and regularly review and apply it in filling the position. This can be done by creating a "Statement of Moral Obligation" which is then reviewed along with the job description and other statements, or it can be incorporated in the job description or elsewhere. Making a separate statement, however, has more impact and is more conspicuous.

C. Church Rules and Policies

Any church policies or rules that will be applied to a position should be formally written and presented to each prospective employee. Rules such as requiring two or more employees to be in attendance in the nursery rather than a single adult, or a rule requiring all new volunteers to belong to the church for six months before working in the nursery or overnight youth programs are good examples of rules that should be written, generally available, and reviewed with all applicants.

IV. SOME PROBLEM AREAS

A. What is a Legitimate "Religious" Preference?

As noted, religious organizations operate under different legal restraints than the secular world. Any organization may discriminate (prefer) based on characteristics other than race if that characteristic is reasonably necessary to perform the job (it will then be considered a "bona fide occupational qualification", or BFOQ), or if discriminatory employee selection can be shown to be a business necessity (the "business necessity exception"). A religious organization may go one step further and discriminate based on its religious tenets. To do this, however, it must show that the discriminatory characteristic is founded upon a religious tenet that is integral to its beliefs. In short, it must be a **bona fide religious** belief and not merely some opinion or preference.

1. Establish the Religious Basis!

When the expectation involves a matter of doctrine, the religious aspect is self-evident. But problems have arisen where the expectation went beyond doctrine and involved some other area of preference which is usually prohibited, such as gender discrimination.

> *Example: A church wants to hire a choir director, and will not hire a woman for the position because an aspect of its religious belief is that women should not have a leadership role over men in the church.*

> *Example: A religion holds a tenet that a woman should maintain a full-time nurturing role when small children are in the home. May a church refuse to consider employing women with pre-school children?*

> *Example: A church refuses to hire divorced and remarried women in its day-care program because of its belief that the Bible prohibits remarriage.*

Are these permissible "religious" preferences", or are they impermissible discrimination on the basis of gender or marital status?

For a discriminatory requirement based on a religious tenet to be supported by the courts, the employer need to be prepared to show that the requirement is founded upon a religious tenet that is integral to its beliefs.

How do you do this?

Do this by documenting the basis for the beliefs through such things as biblical references, church pronouncements, church covenants, resolutions adopted at local, state or national church gatherings, and decisions of the local church body.

2. *Make it clear!*

Simply assuming that members, workers, and applicants know what the organization expects of its members and employees is assuming too much. It is much safer and clearer to outline any expectations that might be applicable to employees, and then go one step further and signify how and why those expectations are related to the religious beliefs—as, for example by referencing them to Scripture or a church covenant or some adopted policy or belief statement of the church. Again, to minimize litigation, clearly outline any such guidelines in a statement of rules and policies, explain their importance, and then consistently review them with every applicant and apply them without exception.

B. When are Job Qualifications Too Sweeping?

What can you legally require as job qualifications?

> *Example: A church requires a college degree for a floor sweeper position it is filling. Allowable? If the church were subject to many typical state and federal labor laws, this would probably not be permitted, since it would not be necessary to handle the traditional duties of the position.*

Outside the uniqueness of the church setting, any job qualification often must be reasonably related to the tasks the job entails. Thus, you could not require a person to be fluent in Chinese in order to be a short order cook in Des Moines. Such a requirement is not really related to the job and has the effect of discriminating against a whole lot of people who could do the job perfectly well. If a college degree is required of all employees, a claim might be made that the organization is racially discriminatory, since fewer minorities hold college degrees. This practice is referred to as having a "discriminatory effect." It is important as a matter of fairness, and sometimes law, that an organization require only those requirements that directly relate to an employee's ability to perform the particular job function. A college degree can be required in other positions such as a teacher. However, the employer must be careful to apply the minimum criteria to all applicants without exception, and the job description must clearly reveal the need for the requirement.

Quite apart from the law, however, a church probably should be careful about routinely requiring generalized minimum standards to be met by all employees. Requiring irrelevant qualifications actually reduces the pool of truly qualified applicants.

V. LEGAL SIGNIFICANCE OF JOB DESCRIPTION

The job description is particularly important legally.

First, since an established job description states, in writing, exactly what skills the church is looking for, the church can respond to any allegations of favoritism or discrimination with the fact that the applicant could not meet the job requirements *as listed in the job description*. If the job requires travel and the applicant has no driver's license or access to adequate transportation, then refusing to hire the person was based on a legitimate job-related requirement.

Second, the job description provides a basis for evaluation of job performance, and if necessary, dismissal of an employee, if he cannot perform the responsibilities set forth in it.

To get the maximum legal protection from a job description and related statements, make sure the following questions have also been addressed:

- What are the skills and characteristics necessary in performing the job?

- Are there characteristics *reasonably necessary* to perform the job which may be discriminatory?

Remember, a suit can always be filed against a church, but its odds of succeeding against the church are greatly diminished by simple preventative measures. The job description and statements described above are invaluable vehicles for this in a number of ways: they clearly state the church's position and reasons for it; they discourage frivolous claims, since the applicant must acknowledge that the church's position had been presented in a systematic manner from the onset; and the documentation itself is easily presented in a church's defense if a claim is filed. Standardized systems are much more believable and persuasive in a court of law, particularly when the rationale behind them appears so clearly on the face of the documents.

VI. PRESENTATION AND SIGNING OF THE JOB DESCRIPTION

It is a good practice to formally present the job description to applicants and have them sign it as evidence that they received and read it. If there are other documents attached to it, like the Statement of Faith, Statement of Moral Obligation, or copies of rules and policies, they should be included in the presentation and signed as well. The employee could not successfully claim lack of knowledge of any of the statements, or that the church applied some arbitrary "religious" standard as a reason for hiring or termination. By utilizing a standard system, the church is prepared for such claims and can quickly address them, rather than spending time and money having to justify its actions later. Having ALL employees understand and agree to (or at least sign) an established policy goes a long way toward justifying an employment decision in a court of law. It is at least clear that the applicant was made aware of the beliefs and expectations of the church.

STEP #2: IMPLEMENTING A RECRUITING PROCESS

> **Summary Step #2**
>
> **It is now important to develop an efficient plan to reach and encourage qualified employees, and employ a means of initial screening so that the time and energy of applicants and the church are not wasted in pursuing unqualified candidates. A careful process will also minimize allegations of impermissible discrimination.**

Now that the job description is complete and the employer knows exactly what skills and qualifications are sought, it's time to *find* that perfect employee.

Carefully considering the job description will give a good indication of not only what is sought, but where the candidates are likely to be found. If the scope of the search can be narrowed to begin with, recruiting costs can be reduced, and a better response can be expected.

I. HOW TO RECRUIT

A. Internal or Outside Recruiting

It is just plain good sense to seek the best candidates for any position, including church positions, wherever they may be found. Many churches typically hire from within the church body and, therefore, do not develop a careful recruiting plan. There are certainly advantages to this internal recruiting, such as the following:

- Internal candidates are better known than strangers.
- Internal candidates will likely have a better knowledge of the real nature of the job.
- They will have an immediate sense of the mission and character of the church.
- The personality fit will be easier to assess with persons who are well known.
- The gifts and skills of the internal candidates may have already been assessed or demonstrated.
- The internal candidate's commitment to the church and to its faith will often have already been evidenced.

There are, however, disadvantages with exclusive internal recruitment:

- Internal candidates may be hired more because of their friends or personal needs than their skills for the task.
- The inbreeding may inhibit new and creative ideas and approaches.
- The assessment process may be difficult because of personal relationships.
- Later dismissal may be much more difficult and cause church dissension.
- An insider's attachment to certain persons may interfere with his performance.
- Inside candidates may be tempted to inappropriately "lobby" with church leaders for jobs.

Some churches have policies in this regard, but most do not. The one area where such policies are common is in regard to associate pastors—where many churches as a matter of policy will not consider an associate for the position of senior pastor. This is usually based on a desire to avoid two things: setting up any competitive situation where an associate may on his own or through others who prefer the associate, seek to "take over" from the senior pastor; and secondly, to avoid a situation where, when there is a vacancy in the position of senior pastor, the associate who has friends and supporters will subvert an important broader search.

Other church positions, however, such as choir director, accompanist, youth director, janitor, or secretary are quite commonly filled from within the church body. Salaries are quite modest, and demands may be high—and the people attracted to such positions are those with a strong commitment to that church. There is nothing inherently wrong with this, but churches should recognize the potential problems and try and function in a way that minimizes the disadvantages.

Most churches probably do most recruiting through word of mouth. While this may be inexpensive and relatively successful, it limits the range of possible candidates, and may even create some legal problems—depending on whether the church is subject to certain statutory prohibitions. If the church is fairly homogenous in ethnic and racial make-up, while the outside community is not, recruiting from within certainly may have discriminatory results. There may be reasons to justify this, such as a policy of only hiring church members (if this can be supported by a religious tenet that is central to the practice of the religion), or a standard policy that the church discriminates unconditionally based upon a prescribed religious faith, and there is no one in the outside community who meets this qualification. If these criteria are used, the organization must be careful to apply them without exception, and make the qualifications clear and well known to all applicants. Again, the use of the job description, Statement of Faith, Statement of Moral Obligation, and statement of rules and procedures may be helpful here, and will convincingly substantiate the church's practices in a court of law.

B. Where to Look

Besides obvious options like the local newspaper and unemployment office, several possibilities might be worth exploring because of the potential for reaching an audience with more natural interests in church work. Among these special audience options would be the following:

- Local Christian radio stations
- Other church newsletters/bulletin boards
- State or local religious newsletters or magazines
- Denominational offices—local and state
- Christian book and music stores

II. ADVERTISING CONTENT

If an advertisement will be used, be as job specific as possible. Clearly label the position, state the minimum job requirements, be positive about the position (After all, you want to sound attractive to those good applicants.), and give directions on how/when to respond. Narrowly defining when to call (e.g., 8:00 a.m. to 10:00 a.m. on Monday) will allow the employer to prepare for the additional phone work rather than handle disruptions all day, and it will also help screen out applicants who aren't interested enough, or not organized enough to call at the specified time. Those applicants may tend to be compulsively late, no-shows, or unreliable, anyway.

III. PROCESSING INQUIRIES - SCREENING

Assuming an effective recruiting plan has been implemented, the next step is handling the inquiries and responses correctly. Failing to qualify applicants before bringing them in to fill out the application or to be interviewed will waste a lot of time. If an applicant is not screened on the phone, no legal snare will be lurking. The employer will simply find itself inundated with less than qualified applicants that it will then have to take additional time to process. The screening process will help avoid this problem--but it must be done correctly in order to avoid discrimination claims.

If your recruiting has indicated that people should phone to respond, which is a good idea, a list of questions should be compiled to help anyone answering the phone to screen applicants. If the applicant continues to be interested and is found to be qualified once the questions are asked, set an appointment for him to come to the employer's site to fill out the job application.

Including the following questions will help avoid wasting anyone's time. Additional questions may be applicable depending on the position, but the following can generally be used for all applicants:

For what position are you inquiring?

- This will clarify quickly if the caller has a clear idea about, and interest in, the specific available position or is a general job seeker. It has the further advantage (if there happens to be more than one position available) of avoiding any allegation that the employer is "steering" some applicants into menial positions based on ethnic voice overtones.

- This question should be repeated on the job application, as discussed later.

We have a policy of hiring only (Baptists, Christians, etc.). Are you still interested?

- Any advertising should include this requirement. This will avoid unnecessary calls.

Do you have reliable transportation to our facility located at _____?

- Do not ask the applicant where he lives, since many towns have areas that are heavily minority occupied and this question may be perceived as discriminatory.

- Many people respond to ads without knowing where the work site is located. Clarifying this will eliminate "no shows" for application appointments.

Are you capable of performing the following job functions?

- Read your job description. This will maintain uniformity.

- Do not ask the applicant if he "has any disabilities or problems." This is a far too general question, and it may impermissibly discriminate against the disabled under the Americans with Disabilities Act. (ADA is discussed later.) But in any event, disabilities should not be relevant unless they impede the applicant's ability to perform the specific job function. In fact, churches may want to be specially sensitive to disabled persons who often find obtaining work difficult.

You will be tested on the following (Include the result that must be scored.).

- Again, test only on those functions directly related to job performance.

- If applicants know they will actually be tested, they will be more likely to eliminate themselves from the process before being weeded out by the test--a time saver for the employer.

- Don't forget to include any medical and drug-testing policies.

IV. POTENTIAL LEGAL ASPECTS OF RECRUITMENT AND SCREENING

We have noted that most churches, due to their size or lack of involvement in interstate commerce, are not covered by many of the federal employment laws. For these churches, the manner of questioning will not result in potential legal liabilities (at least as the law stands today). However, many good applicants are minorities or disabled persons, and the church has nothing to lose and everything to gain by voluntarily following the federal guidelines. Also, keep in mind that the church's image as a caring, upstanding entity can be greatly damaged by its discriminatory practices--whether intentional or not.

However, churches, even if not subject to many federal discrimination laws, may be subject to state or local ordinances which have less exceptions and usually much lower thresholds in terms of number of employees. Some large churches and denominational offices may in fact find themselves subject to some of the federal statutes. It is worthwhile to understand, therefore, the legal aspects in the recruiting and screening context.

Consider this question of law.

A church is located in a community with few minorities, although the surrounding communities are populated by minorities. In answering the inquiries to a receptionist position the church had posted in the local paper, the secretary has been asking callers where they live. The secretary realizes that the pay is low for the position and most people will not want to drive a great distance for that type of pay/position. Also, she anticipates transportation and truancy problems if the receptionist must travel a great distance to the job site. A discrimination suit is filed by a minority who had been screened out (not allowed to apply) by the secretary. Could the plaintiff win this suit?

Certainly, if the employer were a typical business, the plaintiff would have a good argument. Where an employee lives is not related to his ability to perform essential job functions, so it cannot be used as a factor in employment decisions. The secretary should instead address the concerns directly, relaying the approximate pay range of the position, and asking whether the caller has reliable transportation to the job site.

Employment law not only bars direct discrimination, but looks at the <u>effects</u> of employment practices. Certain recruitment practices may have the effect of discriminating against persons without any regard to their ability to do the job. Limiting recruitment to certain select groups, intentionally or unintentionally, may have the effect of eliminating, for example, most minority groups.

Recruiting approaches that MAY have discriminatory effects would include recruiting only in select areas, or in publications which do not represent the diversity of the community. The screening process may also have discriminatory effects, such as in the differential application of standards. Consider this situation.

Example: A female inquires about a posted position and is asked a series of questions, including whether or not she can type 50 w.p.m. In responding "no", she is not given an interview. She learns that her male friend also responded to the ad, was not asked any questions, and was given an appointment to apply for the position. She sues, claiming the employer is discriminating based on gender. Will she win?

Depends. If the typing requirement were only applied to female applicants, she would win. If the typing requirement were listed in the job description and applied to all applicants (whether applicants were informed of the requirement over the phone or in person while applying), the requirement will be considered legitimate, and the suit will fail.

Screening may also have a discriminatory effect if it asks questions which are used to eliminate persons without regard to actual qualifications; or which, for example, tend to impact a minority group. *Do you have a car?* Obviously eliminates a lot of poorer people but may be irrelevant to the actual job.

Remember, there is NEVER a problem with any preference or discrimination based on bona fide religious belief in church hiring, or on the basis of any qualification required to perform the job. If there is a potential liability for some churches, it would be in other areas that might be irrelevant to the church's doctrine and its job, such as race or ethnic origin or age.

STEP #3: THE APPLICATION FOR EMPLOYMENT

> **Summary Step #3**
>
> A well-designed application will elicit information which enables the church-employer to make an initial assessment of skills and capability, and will also provide indicators of potential problems which the church should investigate further. The application should also be drafted to minimize discriminatory or otherwise irrelevant and inappropriate inquiries.

In most employment contexts, certain information cannot be utilized in making employment decisions, and if such information is contained on the application, there is little reason for a jury to believe that it was not in fact used for illegal discriminatory purposes. Thus, in this example, if the employer were subject to the federal statute barring age discrimination in employment, a question about age on the application would invite the suspicion that age may be a factor the employer is considering. You can minimize such risks by eliminating such questions from the application form.

I. THE APPLICATION—KEY DOCUMENT

The application is a key document and step in the hiring process. It is a primary source of information about the applicant in the employer's attempt to match candidates with the skills and abilities sought.

A carefully drafted application will produce much more than technical information. It will alert the employer to special gifts and skills, patterns in a person's work history, and raise appropriate red flags which may call for further inquiry. A good application form, used correctly, can go a long way toward identifying potential problems with applicants. The application is utilized once the employer has created the job description, recruited for the position, and screened applicants. The remaining applicants are then given appointments to come into the employer's office and fill out the application form and other paperwork.

A well-crafted application will reveal several types of very crucial information:

1. Positive indicators —strengths, gifts, experience, skills, interests, reliability
2. Problem indicators—job hopping, lack of experience
3. Puzzles—things to check out—
   e.g., does job hopping reflect performance or personality problems?
4. People—Sources of independent information—
   references, employers, colleagues, educational offices, etc.

II. APPLICATION—DESIGN AND CONTENT

The application form itself should be designed to gather as much information as possible, while not asking too many questions, or the wrong questions, and being deemed discriminatory. To accomplish this, the questions must be broad enough to uncover discrepancies, suspicious circumstances, character traits, or prior actions that might indicate a future danger to other employees or church members. At the same time, the questions must be narrowly tailored to avoid revealing discriminatory information. The organization cannot utilize a hefty list of questions, standard on older applications, that are now considered discriminatory. To reconcile the seemingly opposing demands of acquiring information versus asking too many (usually just wrongly worded) questions, one should consider what *should* be included, next what *may not* be included, and within each category, how to analyze the information effectively to discover as much about the applicant as can be reasonably expected of a potential employer. The following suggested questions should hit most of the areas ripe for litigation for the unwary employer, but any application form should be reviewed by an attorney before being used.

A. Generality of the Application:

Before the specifics of what should be included are discussed, keep in mind that the application form being created should be applicable to all positions. Unless the organization plans to customize an application for each different job (which few have the time or resources to do), the application must be general enough for all positions. From a legal standpoint, this is important because it forces the employer to delete any information which may not be applicable to every position.

> *Example: If the church requires ALL employees to be members of a certain faith, a question regarding the applicant's religion may be included on the application.*

> *Example: If the job description for a maintenance position requires the ability to lift a certain weight, but ability to lift heavy weight is not required for other positions, it should not be included as a general question on the application. If included it could easily be interpreted as an illegal screening devise for handicapped applicants.*

After reviewing all questions on the application for general applicability and deleting those that are not pertinent to every position and all applicants, what screening system can be utilized in place of the deleted information?

First, the job description should be used to indicate any unusual job requirements. The job description will be read to the applicant during various phases of screening, and the interviewer will be taking special care to cover it thoroughly in the interview. Therefore, the information will be revealed at the appropriate time and considered accordingly.

Second, if there are extensive questions that are applicable to a particular position, a separate questionnaire can be created to gather the additional information. Using either of these techniques will allow the employer to gather the necessary information from select applicants without gathering unnecessary--and potentially discriminatory-- information from others.

B. Questions to Include on the Application:

Most of the following questions are standard on any application form. Those that are of critical legal importance or are particularly valuable from a screening point of view will be italicized and followed by a more in-depth discussion.

General Information:

-Name, address, phone
-Social security number
-How long have you lived at your present address?
-What was your prior address and how long did you live there?
-Are you of a minimum legal age to work?
-What position are you applying for?
-Are you looking for full, part-time, or temporary employment?
-What days and hours are you available for work?
-Have you ever been employed by us before?
-Have you ever applied with us before? What position? When?
-Are you being referred to us by a present or past employee of ours?

Prior Work History:

-Are you presently employed?
-May we contact your present employer at this time?
-List all prior employers.
-List title and major responsibilities.
-Who was your immediate supervisor?
-Did you report to other supervisors as well? Please list.
-Please list start/end dates for all positions.
-Please list start/end salaries for all positions.
-Are you eligible for re-hire?
-Why did you leave?
-How many days were you absent from work last year?
-How many days were you late for work last year?
-Have you ever volunteered for or been employed by a church?

Criminal Record:

-Have you ever been convicted of a crime other than a minor traffic offense?
    If so, please explain.
-Are you currently involved in any legal proceedings? If so, please explain.

Military:

-Were you ever in the military? Dates?
-What branch, rank?
-List major responsibilities.
-Reason for discharge? Please explain.

Education:

-Schools attended, degrees, majors, etc.
-Did you graduate from each?
-Special awards, recognition, training, honors

Personal:

-Please describe any additional skills, training, or experience that you feel would better prepare you for this position within our organization.
-Please describe any personal characteristics that you feel better prepare you for this position within our organization.

The next two questions may be answered during your interview if you prefer. Your answer will NOT automatically disqualify you from employment with us.

-Have you ever been a victim of child abuse?
-Have you ever been a victim of sexual abuse?

References:

-Name, company/position, phone, address for business references
-Name, address, phone and years known for personal references
-Please also fill out a separate Reference Release form for each reference listed.

Christian Commitments:

(These would be quite impermissible questions in most employment contexts, but would be common expectations in most churches and legally permissible so long as they were related to the religious values and requirements of the church-employer.)

Note: Each church would have to develop its own questions here based on its beliefs and whether it chooses to require certain beliefs or standards of conduct of all employees. The questions might include any of the following:

-Briefly describe your Christian experience. (Conversion, spiritual growth, etc.)
-What church leadership roles have you held?
-Have you read the church's Statement of Faith, and do you affirm it personally?
-Have you read the Church Covenant, and will you conform your conduct to it?
-Of what church are you a member? Describe your involvement with the church?
-What do you believe are your spiritual gifts?

Other common elements

In addition to the questions, various other elements are common in a detailed application form, including the following: (See discussion below on the meaning of these provisions.)

1. Disclaimer:

This church is an "at-will" employer and employment may be terminated at any time with or without cause. No information distributed or representations made by any representative of this church should be construed as an attempt to alter the "at-will" status of this position unless a contract is entered which specifically addresses and replaces its "at-will" employment status.

_____   _____
Applicant Signature   Date

2. Authorization and Reference Release:

The above information is true and accurate to the best of my knowledge. I understand that false information will be grounds for termination.

I hereby authorize you to verify all information contained on this application with former employers, references, or appropriate personnel or resources. I further authorize that any personnel at the above listed places of employment or reference may disclose any and all information regarding my work history, personal characteristics, salary, work habits, or other areas of importance to this organization.

Furthermore, I waive the right to sue the aforementioned references for releasing such requested information.

I understand this authorization and termination policy and agree to the release and verification of the aforementioned information.

_____   _____
Applicant signature   Date

III. IMPLICATIONS OF QUESTIONS

The above questions are fairly inclusive and a lot may be gleaned from them if the employer knows what to look for. Much of the importance is obvious or will become so once an employer sees how vital this additional information can be in protecting the organization from liability, as well as in protecting members or others from possible harm. Following is a discussion of the more revealing or complex questions.

What is your address and how long have you lived there? What was your prior address and how long did you live there?

The first response to consider is the length of time the applicant has lived at the present address, particularly if the former address was also for a short duration. Although there may be perfectly legitimate reasons for frequent moves (a spouse's job transfers, etc.), frequent moves should prompt some additional questions in the interview.

What the employer is looking for is a pattern of anti-social or unusual behavior. Does the applicant have trouble holding a job? Does the applicant move frequently for pleasure or a new "adventure"? Worst of all, could the applicant be one step ahead of being caught engaged in harmful or illegal behavior? In conjunction with frequent moves, also check for references that coincide with the various locations or that might indicate reasons for the moves. The employer should feel comfortable with the responses before moving on in the interview.

What position are you applying for?

While it usually won't catch churches, this is a deadly trap for many unwary employers. The employment discrimination arena is fraught with law suits claiming that the applicant was "shuffled off" or encouraged to apply for a lesser position because of race, sex, etc. It is a simple matter to avoid this allegation--simply request the applicant *tell the employer* what position is being applied for. Asking the additional question "Are there any other positions you are interested in, and if so, what are they?" will further document that the applicant was given every opportunity to apply for various positions.

Churches rarely have multiple positions open simultaneously so this is less likely a problem even if they were subject to some statutory nondiscrimination duties.

Are you looking for full, part-time, or temporary employment?

This question has significance in a couple of ways. First, it indicates that the applicant has set the limitations on the type of position for which he will be considered. Legally, this means that the employer cannot be accused of offering only part-time employment to this applicant because of some discriminatory factor. Second, it indicates the appropriate "fit" of the applicant for the position. If the applicant indicates "full-time" and the available position is part-time and will probably never be expanded, hiring this employee may result in turnover if the employee were to obtain full-time employment elsewhere (which means new recruiting, interviewing, training, etc.) If the employer feels the position may be expanded to full-time, a candidate who is willing to work only part-time would not be available for the expanded position, and the same turnover may occur. There is no right or wrong answer for most of these questions, just additional information to be noted before selecting an applicant.

What days and hours are you available for work?

Many positions require that a worker be available on weekends or holidays, or involve a significant amount of travel. While most employers generally may not ask if, for example, the applicant has small children, a question reformatted to ask what hours the applicant is free to work will indicate the applicant's ability to meet the time requirements of the job. If the times listed by the applicant are not satisfactory, further discussion should follow in the interview.

Please list your prior supervisor.

The prior supervisor, as opposed to co-workers or others not within the employee's direct line of command, was directly responsible for knowing and evaluating the employee; this person should have the most pertinent information. A personnel department representative rarely has first-hand knowledge of the company's former employees, and is often under strict orders not to reveal any information besides start and end dates to those requesting referrals. Personnel also frequently request that no further inquiry be made of other company employees, which is why personnel should always be the last stop in reference checking. (Review the section on making effective reference checks for additional information.)

Please list other supervisors if applicable.

If an applicant did report to more than one supervisor, each of them should be contacted. There may be two quite different perspectives on the same person, and the more information you can uncover before a hiring decision is made, the better off you will be. Since the person conducting the reference check will also be asking each reference for other secondary sources who knew the applicant, the more names the applicants list for the prospective employer to contact, the better the chances will be that constructive information will be revealed. Also, asking for a listing of all supervisors negates the possibility that the applicant can avoid a poor referral by steering the future employer away from harmful contacts. Again, information is power.

Please list start and end dates for each position held.

This is a quick method for finding "gaps" in employment, or for verifying that there were no gaps. Gaps may indicate that the employee left the position for questionable reasons, was fired, abandoned the position, or had any number of questionable motives. Gaps are also a good lead-in for determining if there were personnel problems which might have contributed to the departure. Personnel problems always raise a red flag.

Please list starting and ending salaries.

This question can be very productive. First, it simply verifies that the applicant is being honest. Second, it may reinforce reasons for job changes. For example, the salary continues to increase with each job move. Third, it is another factor that may be helpful in finding the right match for the position. If an applicant has historically made more money than the position you are filling pays, the job may fill the immediate need for employment but may not be adequate in the long run. Always consider turn-over when filling a position--or you'll get more practice at hiring than you care for!

Are you eligible for re-hire at each place of employment?

Most applicants will be happy to share their side of a story which they fear might come out differently from a former employer's mouth. This question should prompt a discussion if there has been a problem, as well as provide the prospective employer with more information that can be compared with information obtained from prior employers during reference checks. This question is also a general honesty indicator, since most applicants will not care to reveal past employment problems.

Why did you leave each place of employment?

This is basically a continuation of the previous question, but may elicit information on an unhappy employment situation that was not dire enough to require the person to leave--he is thus still technically eligible for re-hire. This question is also designed to reveal patterns. When discussing this question in the interview, does a common pattern of discontent with co-workers arise? Is salary always an issue? Does the person get bored with jobs easily? If you see patterns, either discuss them until there is a satisfactory answer given, or take the unsatisfactory answer under strong consideration before extending an offer of employment.

Have you ever been convicted of a crime other than a minor traffic offense? If so, please explain.

There is a big difference between asking if an applicant has been "convicted" versus "arrested". Since society is supposed to consider people innocent until proven guilty, asking about arrests unfairly assumes guilt. Stick with "convicted" and allow the applicant to explain further. This is obviously an area to pay particular attention to in the interview and when conducting the background check. (Background checks are discussed further under Criminal Record Checks.)

Reason for discharge from the military?

This question is treated in most senses just like information received by any past employer. However, some states have passed laws to maintain the confidentiality of military records, in which case this question would be illegal. Check on the appropriate state law before including it on the application. (North Carolina allows you to ask this question, but an employer may not discriminate based on the applicant's service in the military.)

Have you ever been a victim of child abuse?

Since a large percentage of child abusers were also abused themselves, this question is critical and absolutely must be asked of those interested in working with children in the organization. A church was recently found guilty of negligent hiring because it failed to ask this question--the jury felt it was such a strong indicator of the propensity to abuse that it was "unreasonable" not to inquire about it.

Oftentimes, a church volunteer or employee will progress from one position within the church to another over a period of time. If this question is only asked of those applying for the nursery, but not of those applying for an office position, for example, the person may eventually move into an area that requires interaction with children. The now-trusted employee has never been screened on this question, a potentially dangerous situation. Including this question on the application will ensure that all employees' backgrounds are known, and restrictions can be place in the files where appropriate.

Have you ever been a victim of sexual abuse?

Again, this mirrors the child abuse question, but is more specific. The employer may want to include a notation that answers may be given directly to a pastor/interviewer rather than disclosed on the application form for both this question and the preceding one. A positive answer should not automatically disqualify one from employment, even in a sensitive position, but should be discussed in terms of the statistical higher incidence of abuse by those who have been abused.

Please describe any additional skills, training, or experience that you feel would better prepare you for this position within our organization.

The beauty of using an open-ended question is that it may elicit information that an employer would like to know, but which he could not ask directly. Since the applicant is the one determining what information is important to relay, the employer is free from the constraints of having to determine exactly how to format the question, or who might feel the question had discriminatory undertones for any number of reasons. Not carrying this burden always simplifies things for the employer, and the applicant is also protected because he can simply omit information in this section if he desires.

Open-ended questions may also be useful in offering lead-ins for further questioning, or in allowing the applicant to reveal otherwise undiscovered strengths or weaknesses.

Obviously, this question will also reveal other factors about potential employees. How interested have they been in furthering their educational or job training? Have they continued to develop personally or professionally by seeking out or taking advantage of developmental programs? Since the areas in which the applicant has further or specialized training probably indicates interests in those areas, are these areas compatible with the position being offered? (Another indicator of "fit".)

Please describe any personal characteristics that you feel better prepare you for this position within our organization.

This question is open ended for the same reason as the previous question. However, because the applicant is being asked about personal characteristics, it also allows a look at the applicant's self-perception, indicating possible personal strengths or weaknesses that the employer may want to explore further. A question like this may also indicate whether the applicant likes to work alone (is possibly more task-oriented) or in a group (a "people person"), each characteristic being a better fit for different positions within the organization. This question may also provide the lead-in for discussing interpersonal relations in the applicant's former positions, or reveal anti-social or unusual views on any number of interpersonal topics.

Disclaimer:

The disclaimer is critical. "At-will" employment means that the employer may terminate the employee without cause. This is the historical system in our country and stands for the principle that employers and employees come together "at will," and that just as an employee may terminate his employment at will, so may the employer. While still upheld throughout the U.S., the at-will doctrine has been constrained by a number of recent developments in law. Employment contracts are one way to specifically negate the at-will employment doctrine. These generally require the employer to follow certain termination procedures and usually require that a termination be for "just cause." Employment labels such as "permanent employee" can also be held to negate the at-will doctrine since it implies that the employee will be hired permanently, thus also implying that the employer may not terminate the employee barring extenuating circumstances or cause. "Annual salary," while not negating the at-will doctrine directly, has been held to imply an annual employment contract and thus a contract to employ and pay the employee in annual periods, regardless of the termination before that period expires. If interpreted in this light, the employer will be forced to compensate the employee for the full year, regardless of when the termination occurred.

Even with specific language stating the position is "at-will," the courts have held that the procedures generally followed by the employer in terminating other employees can create an implied contract to follow those procedures in all cases, negating the ability of the employer to later fire employees without cause under the at-will doctrine.

Employing a person "at will" greatly benefits the employer, because it avoids the time and effort spent on verbal and written warnings, write-ups, documentation ("building the file") and termination procedures. In order to protect this right, however, it is important to state clearly in any employee communication, particularly an employee handbook if one is provided, that the information contained within does not constitute a waiver or replacement of the "at-will" doctrine.

"At-will" employment may not be desirable for some positions within the organization. In that case, a clearly written employment contract for that position should be created to overcome the "at-will" doctrine, while the standard paperwork utilized for all other positions should continue to carry the "at-will" verbiage and disclaimer, thus protecting the at-will status of those positions.

Authorization:

The authorization section is vital. There are three main areas covered by this statement.

First, the authorization contains a statement of the truth of the contents. If the applicant signs the authorization, the truth of the contents has been sworn to and if later, falsities are discovered, the employer has unequivocal grounds for dismissal.

Second, the applicant has agreed that falsities may result in termination at the employer's option.

Third, and most vital, the applicant has agreed to allow all of the information contained on the application to be verified by others. It is important to note that all information is covered (Remember that the application contains salary, start and end dates, reasons for termination, etc.) and that any personnel at the above-listed places of employment or reference may make the reference. This gives the prospective employer the latitude to direct inquiries not only to the listed reference, but also to anyone else who might relay useful information within that organization. The authorization is also broad in including not only the information specifically provided on the application form, but "all information regarding my work history, personal characteristics, salary, work habits, or other areas of importance". This gives the prospective employer great leeway in legally obtaining information, and gives the former employer relief from a possible defamation suit by granting a waiver to release the information. This information will be repeated in separate waiver forms so that copies may be sent to former employers without also revealing other information on the application to them. (More on the specifics of this process will be covered under "Signing the Release Forms," and "Reference Checks".)

Asking the above questions should reveal enough about the applicant for the church or organization to perform a reasonable search into the applicant's background, and to feel safe in making a hiring decision. The next quagmire, however, is ascertaining the questions that may *not* be answered in this pursuit, and a default in this area may be just as legally damaging as not gaining the information in the first place.

IV. LEGAL IMPLICATIONS

The application for employment also requires special attention from a legal standpoint. It has implications both in the negligent hiring liability area as well as potential discrimination claims.

A. Negligent Hiring Aspects

Negligent hiring, as we have noted, is becoming a well-known claim against churches who have failed to take reasonable steps to discover information about applicants before they were hired. Child-abuse cases where the perpetrator had prior convictions, embezzlement of church funds by a church financial officer whose previous embezzlement convictions had not been inquired about, and other equally appalling events clearly indicate that the institutions involved did not implement a thorough, standardized application and employment process. Of course, the completed application itself will usually not reveal direct information about serious misconduct, but it will provide enough history, contacts, and references to permit other appropriate inquiries.

Though the number of perpetrators of crimes in religious organizations may be small, the effects on the victims and the church can be enormous. No church has ever admitted that it should have suspected the perpetrator. Without fail, the church and congregation are surprised, appalled, and at first disbelieving that the person could have committed the crime, but a simple and careful system for checking on applicants can often reveal crucial information from the perpetrator's past. Remember, in a negligent hiring claim, a jury can hold a church liable for failing to discover information that could have been discovered by reasonable steps and which might have been used to avoid an injury to someone--and with increasing frequency are doing so.

B. Discrimination Claims Aspects

Just as with the recruiting and screening, the application process may raise complaints that it is discriminatory. Again, recall the limitations on church liabilities for such discrimination, but even given those limits most churches will want to be sensitive to impressions of discrimination even if they are never sued or are legally vulnerable.

The usual discrimination complaints and lawsuits concern questions on the application which in fact or appearance, tend to cause or invite discrimination against, for example, minorities or older persons, or the disabled. Often it is not the actual information which is the problem but how it asked. In any event, problems of this sort may be minimized for both legal and general policy reasons by avoiding certain questions.

C. Questions to Avoid

When determining whether or not a question should be included in the employment application, a good rule of thumb is to look at each question objectively.

First:

> *Is the information being asked directly related to the applicant's ability to perform*
> *   specific job functions? OR*
> *Is the question legitimately related to a job requirement or related to the religious beliefs*
> *   or moral conduct required by the church?*

If not, it would be best to not include it.

Second:

> Does the question tend to seek information that might be used in a discriminatory way, and if so, could that question be more narrowly tailored to eliminate that possibility while still gathering the needed information? If so, then the question may be included, but should be re-written first in the more narrow form.

The organization may be requesting and utilizing application information in a perfectly legitimate way, but the *appearance* of impropriety is very difficult to rebut in a court of law. Be aware of the differing ways questions could be interpreted, and respond accordingly. These preventative measures will go a long way in avoiding legal difficulties. As an illustration of how questions *may* be viewed as discriminatory, following is a list of questions historically asked on applications that are no longer recommended today.

EXAMPLES:

Please check "Miss", "Mrs.", "Ms.", "Mr.".

While a polite interviewer may simply want to address each applicant appropriately, this question could just as easily be viewed differently. From a legal standpoint, it could be seen as a means of identifying each applicant's gender or marital status in order to discriminate against males or females, or against unmarried or married applicants. Neither of these interpretations would relate to the applicant's ability to perform the specific job functions, and would be deemed inappropriate and discriminatory.

Do you have small children?

The information being sought in this case is usually whether the applicant's children will interfere in the applicant's dedication to the job, or ability to work long or odd hours, or to travel. If these are the concerns, then ask for the information more directly. Replace questions about an applicant's having small children with "Are you able to travel X number of days per month, work overtime as needed, or work varying hours as required by the position?". If the answers are "yes," other information is irrelevant and may create liabilities. If any of the answers are no, the applicant has self-eliminated--a far safer outcome from a legal point of view.

Please list your place of birth.

While a standard question on most applications, it can also be considered an indicator of nationality. Since nationality may not be used in employment decisions, be safe and eliminate this question.

Please list your date of birth.

This question should not normally be included on a standard application because for most employers, it is generally illegal to discriminate based on age. If the employer is simply seeking to verify that the applicant is of the legally employable age, state the question "Are you over the age of ___?". If there is another legitimate reason for the question in a particular position, include the question in the interview or supplement instead of on the job application. This will also eliminate the need to customize the application.

Are you a United States citizen?

This question is sticky and can be easily avoided. Since it is generally illegal to discriminate based on nationality, and the only reason the employer would need this information would be to verify that the applicant can legally work in the United States, re-write the question to read "Can you present documents to verify that you are eligible for work in the United States?" This question is safe and attains the information much more directly. The information will be verified when the applicant later fills out the required I-9 form.

Have you ever been arrested?

Asking about an "arrest" may disqualify an applicant for a positive answer, which unduly penalizes the person who may have been arrested but later declared innocent. Replace "arrested" with "convicted." Of course, a positive response requires thorough follow-up and careful consideration. (Further information can be found under Criminal Record Checks later in this Section.)

How many children or dependents do you have?

An applicant's personal family make-up is rarely relevant to his ability to perform a particular job function. If the true concern is over possible travel restrictions or absences from work, ask about his prior absentee or tardiness records. A direct question will yield a more accurate answer as to the employee's ability to meet the job requirements and will do so without the accompanying legal ramifications.

Please state your height, weight.

Physical attributes are generally not pertinent to a person's ability to perform a job function and so should not be inquired about as part of an employer's standard hiring procedure. If there are physical requirements for a particular position, ask the necessary questions separately in the interview or on a supplemental form.

Are you in good health?

The Americans with Disabilities Act prohibits discrimination against those with disabilities, and those with disabilities are defined as those who are "substantially impaired" from performing a major life activity. A general question regarding health may be considered to inquire into these areas; the question should be eliminated to avoid confusion. Medical information may be gathered once a conditional offer of employment has been made. (See Medical Tests later in this Section.)

Are you a smoker?

While this is not a "protected class" under present federal law, several states have enacted laws prohibiting discrimination based on this factor. Since the trend seems to be to protect larger and larger classes of people, keeping questions such as these off the application form is a safer route to take. If the employer were to be sued based on these questions, a lot of time and money would be spent on legal defense work, even if the outcome were favorable. At any rate, consult the appropriate state laws before they are even considered for use on the application form. North Carolina prohibits discrimination based on an applicant's legal activities while off the job-site. You cannot, then ask if an applicant is a smoker.

Of course, if the church has a religious belief that bars smoking (or use of alcoholic beverages, or any other activities) the question may be legitimate. Usually, however, it is best simply to note these beliefs and requirements in one of the church statements supplied to applicants and ask whether the applicant can meet these requirements.

This is just a selection of common questions that are unsafe or questionable for use on your job application form, and oftentimes cannot be included in the interview either (discussed further in later step). Again, carefully scrutinize any question to make sure it is directly related to the performance of the primary job functions, and that the question cannot be interpreted in another discriminatory manner. If it can be, re-examine the information being sought, and tailor the questions to extract only the necessary information.

V. ADMINISTERING THE APPLICATION AND OTHER DETAILS

The completion of the application by the applicant should be done on the employer's site to ensure that the application is filled out by the applicant without assistance. This is also a good way to keep track of the application forms--having an application form floating around out there for anyone's review is just asking for trouble.

Additionally, the acceptance and retention of applications can have legal ramifications in and of itself. The organization should take care to establish guidelines which are uniformly applied; otherwise, applicants will believe that their applications have been refused or discarded randomly-- or discriminatorily, resulting in a lawsuit.

> *Example: A minority woman fills out an application for the church receptionist position even though no opening has been posted. The following year the woman finds out that a non-minority has been hired by the church as a receptionist. On further inquiry, she finds that her application is no longer on file. She claims that the church discarded her application and discriminated against her because of her race. Does she have a claim?*
>
> *Probably not if the church has a policy of accepting all applications and keeping them on file for twelve months, and then systematically purging ALL unconsidered applications. In this case the church may have justifiably purged her application after twelve months and then begun a new search later for the receptionist position. The church's case will be strongest if they can document the process and show that it is followed consistently.*

One way for the organization to avoid controversy over whose application may have been kept or not kept is to refuse to accept applications if the organization is not actively trying to fill a position. Once the organization recruits for a position, it should then keep all applications on file until the position is filled, and then hold all of the application files of those not selected for twelve months.

If an organization is going to accept applications on an on-going basis, create a standard policy and stick to it. One method is to accept all applications, date them as to the month (not day) received, and routinely throw away the entire batch twelve months later, on say the first of that month. If a position does open, the file can be reviewed for qualified applicants, but the requirements of the job description will be the basis upon which the applications are eliminated, not random review of the applications and the selection of a few who might be good for some future, unforeseeable position. Random retention could easily be viewed as selecting only those of a particular race or sex and discarding the rest.

Whichever method is chosen, do be aware that the system must be systematically applied, and, ideally, should also be explained in the "Church Rules and Procedures" (See Step #1.) for clarity. This will prevent misinterpretation by applicants, and will provide firm documentation should it ever be required. (For further information on retaining records, see Step 10, this section.)

STEP #4: OBTAINING SIGNED RELEASE FORMS

> **Summary Step #4**
>
> **Churches should obtain signed release forms from applicants. This will greatly assist the church in obtaining key information from prior employers and others, and thus help minimize risks of negligent hiring allegations.**

If a church releases information on a former employee to a prospective employer, can the church be held liable for defamation if it relayed information regarding the employee's personality, including his inability to get along with others?

No. Employers are protected by a "qualified privilege" which allows them to relay information in the regular course of business to a prospective employer, assuming it is not relayed with malice.

I. THE NECESSITY OF REFERENCE CHECKS—YET RESISTANCE BY PRIOR EMPLOYERS

Since an organization can be held liable for negligent hiring if it does not reasonably discover pertinent information about an employee, it must conduct thorough and consistent record and reference checks on all potential employees. On the other hand, in our litigious society there are more and more defamation claims being filed by employees who object to the sharing of information--suits which are costly to defend even if the organization relaying the information is in the right. This results in employers being reluctant to share valuable information on their former employees--an outcome that is destructive to all employers, because it minimizes the available information that can be considered in a hiring decision.

In order to gather crucial information about potential employees while at the same time protecting employers from lawsuits, the organization must first incorporate measures to increase the productivity of reference checks, and, second, increase the protection it can offer against negligent hiring claims and defamation suits. A few simple steps will accomplish this goal.

Keep in mind that good employees welcome record and reference checks because they present another opportunity for them to reinforce their credentials and fitness for a position. They will quickly sign the proposed reference forms. Applicants with something to hide, on the other hand, resist offering negative information, and often will leave very few clues to follow in allowing a prospective employer to conduct the reference and record checks--which makes it particularly critical for a productive check to be made. These are also the employees who are most likely to bring defamation claims in order to challenge a former employer or to use the threat of litigation to quell the former employer's willingness to share information on that employee. During a reference check, former employers can sound an alert for all types of potential problems and dangers, but getting the information from them is often difficult.

II. THE "QUALIFIED PRIVILEGE"

Since the biggest barrier in getting and sharing employee information is overcoming the fear of a defamation suit, it is important to be familiar with the protection available from these suits under the "qualified privilege" for employers.

The "qualified privilege" is designed to foster the sharing of information among employers. If information is released in good faith and in the regular course of business to a prospective employer (meaning that both the conveyor and the conveyee have an interest or duty in the matter relayed), it is considered a privileged communication. In order for the employee to overcome this protection, the employee must then prove that the information was given with "malice." This is a difficult hurdle for the employee to overcome, since a malicious comment is defined legally as one made with knowing falsity, in bad faith, or with reckless disregard for the truth.

Besides the employer privilege, there are two other defenses an employer has to a defamation claim. Truth is always a defense. If the information relayed is indeed truthful, it is not defamatory. Second, consent is a defense. If the employee signs a statement that he consents to the release of information, he cannot later sue the employer for releasing it (hence, the importance of the waiver, discussed more fully below).

There is also a privacy issue when gathering information. A potential employer should only ask for information pertinent to making a hiring decision, and that information should be recorded and filed in the applicant's file. Only those persons who need to know such information should have access to it. Allowing others to see this information might constitute an invasion of the applicant's rights of privacy.

> *Example: A reference relays the fact that a former employee created disturbances, had frequent conflicts with other employees, and was finally fired. The employee sues the former employer for defamation. Will the suit succeed?*
>
> *No. First, the communication was privileged, and assuming there was no malice involved, cannot be sued upon. Second, the information relayed was truthful, and is thus not considered defamatory. Third, the employee signed an authorization allowing the information on the application to be verified, and thus consent can be used as a defense.*

Considering the many available defenses, in the normal course of events, employers should feel free to exchange information, thereby protecting the public by seeing that dangerous information is relayed to future employers as needed. However, this does not seem to be the case.

Why are employers reluctant to share this information? Most organizations are not aware of their legal right to relay negative information, are afraid of having to defend a suit of this type, or are concerned that an employee may in fact make a comment maliciously--an employer can't predict nor prevent every comment made by every employee in the organization. The organization therefore institutes a standard policy of not sharing information to ensure that all possible problems are avoided.

Example: An employer allows employees to use their own discretion in giving referrals when requested. A prospective employer randomly reaches an employee who had an active dislike for the former employee, and who relays false and malicious information. The former employee sues for defamation. Could this suit succeed?

Probably. The former employer could have protected the company from suit by instituting a policy of not releasing information. The employee would then have been acting outside the scope of his/her employment in relaying the information--this is a common route for companies today. The company would also be free from liability if a release form had been requested beforehand (since consent is always a defense to defamation), particularly if the release included a waiver of the right to sue. (This route protects the employer as well as allowing the free exchange of information.)

III. UTILIZING RELEASE FORMS

A. Components

One way to overcome and minimize this problem of prior employer resistance to sharing information is the use of reference release forms. A good reference release form is a statement signed by the applicant which covers three areas of concern:

- it authorizes the prospective employer to converse with any employees of the named company;

- it authorizes the prospective employer to discuss any relevant information with references;

- and, it includes a waiver of the right to sue the former employer for disseminating such information.

Good employees will not object to a waiver of this type. Potentially dangerous employees will probably remove themselves from consideration for a position once he realizes that a thorough check will be made. Consider the importance of each part of the waiver below.

FIRST, the release should authorize the prospective employer to contact not only those individuals listed on the reference form, but also anyone within that particular business or organization. This will allow the prospective employer to ask the listed reference for "secondary references" (discussed further under "Effective Reference Checks"), who might offer a different opinion of the employee than the first reference did. This will also effectively circumvent the applicant's ability to steer a future employer to selected references within a company, while avoiding damaging input from others. This will increase the likelihood that the person with the most information will actually be reached.

The **SECOND** item included in the release form is the authorization for the prospective employer to contact prior employers for all *types* of information. The release should list such items as personality, work habits, punctuality, work quality, employee relations, or other areas that might be of concern in hiring an applicant to perform a particular function. This addition will preclude claims that the employer abused the employer privilege by relaying information that was not related specifically to the job function, since the reference release constitutes a consent of the release of all listed information. This type of inclusion is particularly useful for a church or religious organization which may request more personal information than a secular employer usually requests. Having the inclusion will be important since employees and juries may view such unusual requests suspiciously.

> *Example: A potential employer contacts a former employer who has been listed as a reference. In the course of the conversation, the potential employer asks if the rumor concerning the applicant's mother being a drug addict is actually true, and receives a response. The applicant sues for defamation. Could this suit succeed?*

> *Generally, yes. A communication of this type falls outside information deemed "privileged," since it does not concern a matter that both parties have a duty or interest in. However, if the applicant has signed a release form allowing such communications, he/she cannot then bring suit based upon them.*

The **THIRD** item that must be included is the waiver of the employee's right to sue the former employer for defamation for relaying information. This is really most important to the former employer, who then has a greater zone of comfort in which to answer questions. Since the waiver is written and signed on a separate sheet for each listed reference, the sheet can easily be faxed or mailed to the previous employer before the reference check proceeds. Ideally, the reference will be contacted, the fact that the waiver has been signed will be discussed, a copy will be sent or faxed to the previous employer, both the prospective and previous employer will file the form for future reference, and the discussions will proceed in a more open and informative manner, resulting in the potential employer's acquiring critical information the former employer would not have otherwise relayed. This form can work wonders in overcoming the "no comment" mentality prevalent with employment checks today.

> *Example: An applicant applies for a position and the potential employer contacts the applicant's references. One of the references mistakes her for another employee and relays that the applicant had been fired. The applicant sues the former employer for defamation. Will the applicant win?*

> *No. Since the information relayed by the employer was privileged, the employee would have to prove that the incorrect information was relayed with malice. Assuming there are no other facts to consider, a simple mistake will not meet the malice requirement, and the suit would fail.*

This rounds out the available protections. The employer now has a right to speak to each and every employee, and to ask the desired questions; and if for some reason a problem arises, the employee has waived his right to sue. An employer operating in good faith should not need these additional protections, but they will still be invaluable in preventing frivolous claims and in eliciting critical information from others.

B. Incorporating and Utilizing the Reference Release Form

First, list the Form on the face of the actual application. This will screen immediately anyone that has something damaging in his background. It will also alert the applicant to the depth of the check that will be made, thus encouraging cooperation in the listing of helpful information. Including the release form on the application will also put the applicant on notice of the requirement that all applicants sign the form and of the legal rights that are being waived. If an applicant has a problem signing the form, there is probably good reason--a good indicator of problems that the potential employer should feel lucky to have avoided!

Second, the applicant should also sign a brief individual form with information duplicating that on the application. The particular reference to be checked should be listed on the form, along with appropriate phone numbers, addresses, and individuals to be contacted. This form is important not only for the reasons discussed above (offering a way past the traditional "no comment" from prior employers; and the prior employer and prospective employer will have a signed copy for their files should the employee ever attempt legal action), but because it gives the church or organization clear and convincing evidence that it did everything possible to obtain background information on prospective employees and to hire with utmost care. This would certainly surpass the "reasonable" standard of action required to avoid a negligent hiring claim.

Employment Application (excerpt from):

Authorization and Reference Release:

The above information is true and accurate to the best of my knowledge. I understand that false information will be grounds for termination.

I hereby authorize you to verify all information contained on this application with former employers, references, or appropriate personnel or resources. I further authorize that any personnel at the above listed places of employment or reference may disclose any and all information regarding my work history, personal characteristics, salary, work habits, or other areas of importance to this organization. (Each employer should further customize this list.)

Furthermore, I waive the right to sue the aforementioned references for releasing such requested information.

I understand this authorization and termination policy and agree to the release and verification of the aforementioned information.

_____   _____
Applicant's Signature   Date

Reference Release Form

Reference:

_____
Company (if applicable)

_____
Address

_____
Phone

_____
Contact   ext.

_____
Contact   ext.

_____
Contact   ext.

_____
Contact   ext.

I hereby authorize (name of church), (city), (state), to verify all information contained on this application with former employers, references, or appropriate personnel or resources. I further authorize that any personnel at the listed places of employment or reference may disclose any and all information regarding my work history, personal characteristics, salary, work habits, or other areas of importance to this organization. (Each employer should further customize this list.)

Furthermore, I waive the right to sue the aforementioned references for releasing such requested information.

I understand this authorization and termination policy and agree to the release and verification of the aforementioned information.

_____   _____
Applicant's signature   Date

Summary Step #5

A church should employ appropriate skill testing and, depending on the nature of the position, medical and personality tests may be appropriate, but these are rather controversial. Drug testing is growing in the general employment arena, but probably is less critical in most church positions.

A woman responded to an advertisement for a church administrator. After filling out the application, she was given a "job predictor" test. One week later, she received notice that because the test had "predicted" that she would not succeed as a church administrator, she had been eliminated from consideration for the position. She sued the church claiming sex discrimination after noting that most of the people holding managerial positions within the church were men. Could she succeed?

Possibly. If the test has not been validated to ensure that it predicts what it says it will predict, and that it is not biased against minority classes, she may have a good case. If, on the other hand, the test has been extensively statistically validated, the church will have a strong defense for its use.

I. TESTING: THE SEARCH FOR OBJECTIVE CRITERIA

Every employer struggles with the elusiveness of finding the "best" employee. Everything seems so subjective. References, applications, interviews—they rarely provide the kind of definitive answers many employers would like.

Thus, it is not surprising that employers of all sorts have turned to others for help, and especially they have sought to find "tests" which could give some more objective indications for comparing applicants and judging probable job success. How good is the person? How well can they really type? How will they fit in here? Is this a team player? Testing to find answers to some of these questions has become increasing common, and it takes many forms:

Traditional Types:
 Skills testing: e.g., typing test, dexterity, spelling and grammar
 Medical testing: health status

More Recent :
 Drug testing

More Controversial:
  Psychological profiles
  Job Success indicators

II. TESTING: A PROBLEM AREA

Testing is an area that includes skills testing, personality and "job success predictor" tests, medical exams, and tests to detect foreign substances (drugs and alcohol). The testing arena is more or less controversial, depending on what type of test is being given. Skills testing, for example, is much less controversial than personality tests. Medical examinations and substance testing can also be relatively safe if the proper policies are established ahead of time.

Two common terms in the testing field are "bias" and "validation." *Bias* refers to the outcome of the test being consistently lower for a minority group than for others. *Validation* refers to the extensive, time consuming evaluation process that determines whether the test will actually measure what it says it will measure and that it does so consistently and accurately. Bias is usually a problem with cognitive skills tests (such as comprehension, spelling, problem solving) rather than manual dexterity tests (such as typing). To correct for this, some tests require the administrator to adjust scores based on factors such as race or gender. A statistically validated test will take into account all such problems and will have addressed and corrected for them. These are the safest tests to use and are usually available from reputable companies whose sole business is developing and validating such tests.

Each type of test considered for use requires special consideration in selection and administration, and each has unique legal ramifications for the unwary user. Be aware of the possible pitfalls in each area, and adopt measures accordingly.

III. SKILLS TESTING

Skills testing can be one of the safest and most useful types of testing if selected and applied properly. Because hiring decisions should be made based on an applicant's ability to perform essential job functions, the test should measure a skill that is essential to the performance of the job function. It should be easy to determine where a test is appropriate once a job description is created. If typing, for example, is not listed in the job description as an essential function of a position, then a typing test would be inappropriate since the results could not be used to select a candidate.

> *Example: A gentleman applies for an office position. He is given proficiency tests on a variety of office equipment even though the bulk of the job involves computer work. The job is later given to a woman. The gentleman claims the tests were discriminatory because they "weed out" men, who tend to have fewer general office skills than women. Does he have a legitimate claim?*
>
> *Possibly. If proficiency in using the office equipment being tested on is not essential in performing the job, the tests may be inappropriate. If they are essential, the church may require the testing even if it has a disparate impact on men, and the claim will fail.*

IV. JOB "SUCCESS PREDICTOR" TESTS

This type of test is used to determine if someone has the right "personality" to succeed in a given position. Many companies use such tests before promoting an individual and some use them before the initial hiring. Such tests can create legal difficulties because of their propensities for abuse: it is hard to tell if they are accurate; it is hard to discern if they measure a skill necessary to the essential functions of the job; and, because of their seemingly unrelated series of questions, those taking the test often wonder what the "right" answers were--it leaves doubt in the applicant's mind as to the legitimacy of the test.

These types of tests are much more applicable for administrative, managerial and pastoral positions. These positions require multi-dimensional skills, and personality traits are often closely linked to effective job performance. Many of these personality traits are not easily assessed by typical application questionnaires. Because of the central importance of these positions, maximum care should be given to employment decisions. In this context some churches, and most denominational state or national offices, utilize a broad range of means in evaluating candidates often including psychological and "success predictor" tests. These are discussed in more detail in the chapter on pastoral hiring.

Some critics of such personality tests wonder about the underlying assumptions of the test creators, and whether such tests would not in fact find some of the greatest church leaders "unqualified" or at least "risks." Would the Apostle Paul have fallen within the medians of a personality test? Would he not possibly have scored dangerously high in categories our society finds troublesome? One of your authors recalls the personality test given on entering seminary, and a question on it: "Do you think you are a secret agent of God?" Consistent with his theology he answered "Yes," believing he was indeed called as an agent of God. Of course, this was not the answer the test creators thought was a "healthy" response.

V. MEDICAL TESTS

This area includes all required medical tests and physical exams. The first potential problem to note is that in many contexts, the exam may not be lawfully conducted *before* an offer is extended. However, the offer may be contingent on the exam being passed.

Further, it is also impermissible to gather certain medical information before a conditional job offer is made. While it is permisssible to ask the applicant if he can perform essential functions of the job, it is not permissible to seek information about particular problems such as disabilities (AIDS, for example) unless the conditional job offer has been extended. The "condition" of the conditional job offer may be the satisfactory passing of medical tests that address job-related qualifications.

The second problem is that the applicant may claim that the employer who denied him a position based on the results of the exam was unqualified to make such a determination. This can be simply avoided by leaving such a determination to the physician. If the position involves extensive lifting, for example, the job description should state the amount of weight, frequency of lifting, and any further details that would assist the physician in assessing the applicant's ability to meet the job requirements. The physician would then be requested to sign a statement as to the applicant's ability perform these functions. Any further action would be based on this determination.

Example: A gentleman is hired as the church office manager contingent on his passing a physical exam. After failing a stress test, he is rejected for the position. He sues, claiming his chronic heart condition is a disability protected by the ADA. Can he win?

Not if the church can show that the ability to perform under heavy stress/duress is an essential function of the job. Allowing requirements of this sort protects both the applicant from injury and the church from hiring someone who will be physically unable to perform in the position.

VI. SUBSTANCE TESTING

Substance testing includes testing for both alcohol and drugs. It is perfectly acceptable to refuse to hire a candidate who tests positive for an illegal substance (drugs), but in some states it is illegal to refuse to hire someone who tests positive for a legal substance (alcohol or cigarettes/nicotine) used on non-company time. (North Carolina has such a law, so a positive alcohol or nicotine test could not be the basis for a secular employer's refusing to hire someone.) Other states don't offer this protection, so employers could, for example, refuse to hire smokers.

A religious organization may also, however, discriminate based on alcohol or other *legal* substances if the use of such substance is contrary to a religious tenet, such as the forbidden use of caffeine, cigarettes, or alcohol. If this is the case in your organization, list such a policy in the Church Rules and Policies, Statement of Faith, or in the Statement of Moral Obligation so the policy can be easily explained to applicants and shown to be applied uniformly.

A recovering alcoholic or drug abuser is handled differently under the law than an active drug or alcohol user. Active substance abuse is never protected, so a positive drug test can always be grounds for refusing employment with no further justification. If the applicant admits to being a "recovering" or "former" substance abuser, however, the American with Disabilities Act (ADA) considers this a "disability," and employment cannot be denied based upon it. This Act is troubling to many religiously-affiliated organizations and churches because of its definition of a disability, and, specifically, the tendency to treat certain areas related to conduct, such as drug addiction and alcoholism, as "disabilities." The extent to which the Act's inclusion of these controversial areas will be imposed on a religious community is at present unclear. Certainly where the ADA's imposition would burden a sincerely held religious doctrine, there would be a constitutional challenge.

Active alcohol use, though alcohol is not an illegal substance, can be prohibited in the workplace. If an applicant is going to be randomly or regularly tested for drugs or alcohol, make sure he is aware ahead of time that a positive result will be grounds for termination. This, along with the established rules and policies, will help avoid the contention that the church was unfair or arbitrary in its testing, policies, or dismissals.

Again, the biggest precaution to take with both legal and illegal substance testing is to establish a policy regarding these substances ahead of time and to apply it consistently. If the church will refuse to hire anyone with a positive result, such policies should again be included in your "Church Rules and Policies" and provided to persons as part of the Job Description package. This will alert applicants that such tests will be performed, giving applicants an opportunity to self-eliminate before time and money is wasted on testing.

Skills, success predictor or personality, medical and substance tests can be good tools in acquiring information and selecting the right applicants for a job. They can also help quantify capabilities and substantiate decisions made in the hiring process. A church should, however, take care to address the concerns listed above before implementing such tests and should regularly review changes in job requirements and technology to make sure the tests being given remain appropriate.

STEP #6: CONDUCTING INTERVIEWS

> **Summary Step #6**
>
> **The interview should be a carefully planned conversation, with specific goals in mind, and not merely a casual, too often rambling dialogue. A properly focused interview will elicit key information and assist the church in evaluating the applicant.**

The interview is obviously one of the most useful steps in selecting a good applicant for a position; but if not performed correctly, it can also be a useless process, or even worse, it may even give rise to legal liability. The following suggestions will assist the employer in conducting a good interview and in avoiding potential liability.

I. PREPARING FOR THE INTERVIEW

The interviewing process begins before the applicant ever arrives, because the interview should be a natural progression in the hiring process, continuing the line of questioning and information gathering begun in the prior phases. It should not be a rambling "chat" session. If the interview process begins, as is too often the case, with the interviewer grabbing "the file" on the way in to meet the applicant, the entire process is not likely to be very helpful.

First, carefully review the job application. Note any gaps in employment, reasons for leaving past employers, "patterns" of behavior, positive or missing responses to sexual or child abuse questions, and any interesting information offered under "personal characteristics", "skills", or other categories. Create a list of questions or concerns that come to mind related to these responses.

Second, prepare a customized interview questionnaire for the position being filled. This will include questions which will be asked in addition to those compiled from the application form and will insure that all appropriate information is gathered from each applicant. The form will also make it easier to compare applicants afterward, since the same information will have been accumulated on each. Selecting the questions for the interview requires a lot of thought. These questions should be open-ended so as to invite feedback from the applicant, while still dictating what type of question will be addressed. (See examples of suggested questions at end of this section.)

Third, the final step in preparing for the interview will be to compile all of the above questions into a workable interview form, taking care to include an area for comments. Responses not solicited by the interviewer, unexpected information given, and the interviewer's impressions and notes will be recorded here. This will further standardize the information gathering, prompt the interviewer to record all pertinent information, and provide documentation of the interview proceedings, should such documentation ever become necessary.

II. CONDUCTING THE INTERVIEW

During the interview itself, the applicant should do most of the talking. The interviewer certainly will begin and direct the exchange, and "keep control" of the interview. Otherwise, the interview may be too long, too short, unfruitful, or result in required information not being gathered. But the interviewer should try and make sure the applicant is active—expressing his strengths and interests, and responding fully to questions.

Review Job Description

After introductions and pleasantries are exchanged and the applicant seems comfortable, begin the exchange with a review of the job description. Ask if there are any essential job functions that the applicant cannot perform. If the applicant has a disability, ask enough information to discern whether or not a reasonable accommodation may be made to permit the person to fill the position. The Americans with Disabilities Act requires covered employers to make "reasonable accommodations" for a disabled person to allow him to perform a job despite the disability. The employer must make this accommodation unless such accommodation would create an undue hardship for the employer, or unless making the accommodation would affect an essential job function. Do not continue to inquire into a disability beyond its effect on the applicant's ability to perform the essential job functions. Also, any notes taken in this regard should be strictly stated in terms of the job description and the essential functions of the job. Further information found in a file may be deemed discriminatory.

> *Example: A disabled person interviews for a church position. The interviewer is interested in his disability and questions him extensively, asking what other types of social, physical, and non-job related activities he is unable to perform. The applicant is not hired, and later sues for discrimination under the ADA. Will his claim succeed?*
>
> *If the applicant was otherwise qualified and could perform the essential functions of the job, the listing of other non-job related information looks highly suspicious and could convince a reasonable jury that the disability was indeed the reason the applicant was not chosen. Leave information not directly related to the applicant's ability to perform the job out of the interview, and certainly out of the records.*

Raise Issues/Questions from Application

Cover the questions or concerns derived from the application next. Applicants appreciate finding that the interviewer did indeed read what was written, and will likely be forthcoming with explanations. If he is not forthcoming, or the answers are not satisfactory, make such note and move on.

Other Standard Questions

The standard questions will be used next. This will standardize (somewhat) the interviews so that applicants can be more easily compared, and will ensure that the interviewer requests all of the necessary information. Unique or questionable responses can be delved into more fully as the interviewer proceeds, but all questions should be addressed before the close of the interview.

Concluding the Interview

At the close of the interview, thank the applicant for his time and interest in the position. Let him know what to expect next, whether it will be a second interview, further testing, or a decision. Give the applicant a time frame, if possible. This will decrease the number of inquiry calls in the following days or weeks while a decision is being reached.

Post-Interview Steps

After walking the applicant to the door, return your attention to the file and document any further thoughts on the interview while the interview is still fresh in mind. Finally, review all of the notes made during the interview from an objective point of view. Were observations made and responses recorded using clearly non-discriminatory language? Would others interpret any entries as discriminatory? If there is anything questionable, elaborate and clarify it before the file is closed. This extra step will pay off if a suit is ever filed.

III. MULTIPLE INTERVIEW CONTEXTS

In many church employment situations, there may be multiple interviews, or at least contacts. For example, a choir director applicant may be expected to interview with the personnel committee, the pastor, the music committee, and, perhaps, the choir or representatives. A pastoral candidate may meet not only with the search committee, but with deacons or other representatives of the church before final selection. Day-care work applicants may meet with a personnel committee, but also with other staff.

In these situations, the multiple contacts are sometimes intended to be additional formal interviews, and in others more on the order of a chance for further mutual exposure, with the expectation that if red flags emerge from subsequent contacts, the principal interviewing group will be contacted.

In these situations, it is important to make sure that both the candidate and the various groups involved understand their roles, and what is expected of them. If, for example, the initial interviewing group/person assumes the pastor will handle inquiries about spiritual commitments, that ought to be clear to the interviewers.

There should also be an established means for the various groups who interview or have contact to report their observations, opinions, questions, etc., so that information will be accumulated by one responsible source. Keeping all information and input in the applicant's file should handle this for you.

IV. DOCUMENTATION—LEGAL AND PRACTICAL VALUES

It is crucial that any employer keep accurate records of the employment process, including notes from the interview. From a practical point of view, such notes made before, during and after the interview assure a thorough process and provide a record that can be consulted when it is time to compare applicants and make final decisions. If there are many applicants it is easy to forget specific applicants' strengths or weaknesses. Good notes taken during the interview and post-interview reflections greatly aid the evaluation process.

Legally, such documentation is crucial in establishing the nature and scope of the employment process and the factors that were inquired about, weighed, etc. This is crucial information if someone later alleges either some impermissible discrimination, or claims some negligence in hiring. If the documents, for example, clearly show that the church made reasonable inquiries into certain matters, the church's case against a negligent hiring suit will be greatly strengthened. Without such records, we are often left with uncorroborated testimony of people with conflicting stories, and often rather vague memories of what really happened.

Proper documentation should not contain any discriminatory information. Just as the interviewer must be careful to phrase questions in a non-discriminatory way, so must equal care be taken in recording interview events.

Example: A young lady applies for a receptionist position. After not receiving the job, she files suit. She claims that the church was discriminatory in not hiring her due to her obesity. It is later discovered that the interviewer noted her appearance as "unfit," "unappealing," and "not attractive," though her other qualifications were noted as excellent. Could she have a claim?

Probably. Even though the church's comments were actually directed at the fact that the plaintiff showed up for the interview in torn, cut-off blue jeans and a T-shirt, had unclean, unkempt hair, and emitted an awful body odor, the jury may easily believe that the applicant was not hired due to her weight. To avoid misrepresentation, the notes should have more specifically noted the attire and state of uncleanliness, in which case the applicant's claim would have failed.

STEP #7: CHECKING REFERENCES

> **Summary Step #7**
>
> It is essential to identify persons who can provide vital information about applicants, and then to develop a means of securing accurate and revealing evaluations from these sources. In the modern context, many are reluctant to reveal what could be very essential information. The employer must carefully plan how to secure the cooperation of references.

A church attempts to perform a reference check on a gentleman being considered for a managerial position with the youth ministry program. The church contacts all three former employers listed on the job application, but all three refuse to relay any information besides the start and end dates of employment. The church proceeds to hire the individual, but does not note that the reference checks were attempted. A youth group member's parent later sues the church for negligent hiring after the gentleman attempts to accost a youth. Could this claim succeed?

Possibly. If the employee had either a criminal or prior work record of such abuse and the parent could convince the jury that a "reasonable" check had not been made into such records, the claim would probably succeed. If the church had conducted a criminal record check (assuming it came back negative) and the proper reference checks, and further documented either its unsuccessful attempts at acquiring the information or the negative results of the attempts, the church would have a strong defense, and the suit would fail.

I. IMPORTANCE OF REFERENCE CHECKS

The reference check is perhaps the most frustrating and dreaded step an employer takes in hiring an individual. Because of the fear of a defamation suit or other repercussions from a former employee, many employers refuse to give any but the most factual and scant information to someone conducting a reference check. Some employers today will only give the dates of the person's employment such as "Mr. _____ was employed by _____ from March 15, 1991, to December 5, 1993." This is obviously not very helpful.

However, should a forthcoming prior employer be reached, the information relayed may prove to be the most valuable, insightful information available to a prospective employer--information which may be irreplaceable in preventing injury and later legal suits against the church. For this reason, it is well worth an employer's time to learn to effectively conduct a reference check and to implement systems to overcome the barriers and obtain the necessary information.

A reference check takes time and effort by both the party seeking and the party giving information. For this reason, it should be one of the final steps in the hiring process, reserved only for those applicants a church would hire pending a positive reference check.

II. STEPS IN A REFERENCE CHECK

A. *Step #1: Preparing the documents.*

To begin, gather the following documents which will be used to prepare and to conduct the reference check:

- the job application
- the job description
- any applicable statements of faith, moral obligation, or Church Rules and Policies
- a list of questions (after adding additional questions applicable to this position)
- the Reference Check Form on which the answers will be documented
- and, the signed Reference Release Form for that employer

Next, review the Reference Check Form for questions which may be deleted, and for questions which may be pertinent to a particular position which may need to be added. There is space in the second set of questions to add them. (See example in Appendix.)

Careful preparation, particularly in formatting the questions to be asked, is critical in performing a productive reference check. If the appropriate questions are not asked, even an interview with a cooperative prior employer will not reveal critical information, and injury and corresponding legal trouble may result. Likewise, if the prospective employer is not prepared to carefully document responses, the church will not be able to effectively defend itself should such trouble actually arise.

The questions asked of the prior employer will serve three purposes.

First, the information given by the reference will verify the information given on the application.

Second, the applicant's skills and abilities as they pertain to the particular position will be confirmed.

Third, if at all possible, personal information, work habits, etc., of the applicant will be delved into, which may reveal information or problems that the application had not addressed, personal perceptions of the employer, or other valuable information. For much of the information requested, the references are the only source.

B. *Step #2: The initial contact.*

To conduct the actual reference check, contact the listed reference, identify yourself and your church, and the reason for your call. Tell the reference that you have a signed reference release form that allows references to reveal any and all pertinent information, as well as a waiver of the applicant's right to sue the reference for relaying such information. Offer to fax or send the reference form immediately. Some references may hesitate to answer any questions until the document is received. If this is the case and the mail will be used, estimate the time needed for the release to arrive and set a convenient time to re-contact the reference in order to continue the reference check.

If the reference is still unwilling to address the questions, ask for a written confirmation of this refusal. If the reference will not prepare something for you, ask if he would be willing to sign and return a form which you will prepare and mail to them. At any rate, attempt to have the reference person document the refusal. If impossible, prepare the documentation yourself and include it in the personnel file. Be as complete and thorough as possible in defining the chain of events. Although such a refusal is not helpful in acquiring information about the applicant's background, documentation will be vital in defending the "reasonableness" of the employer's actions should the applicant be hired and a later problem arise. The self-documentation might look like this:

_____
Applicant's name

_____
Reference Contacted

On (date), I contacted the above named reference in regard to the employment application of the person named above. I spoke with _____, and identified myself and the purpose of my call.

He/She did advise me that ....(Note information provided such as dates of employment, reason for termination of employment or whatever IS told.)

I requested information regarding ......(Note specific questions or areas—you may do this by reference to certain questions on the Reference Check Form.)

The person refused, however, to provide such information, even though I offered to provide them a Release Form signed by the applicant. They also declined to sign any form indicated they were declining to provide this information. The reason they gave for refusing to provide such information was (e.g. "company policy," "privacy" etc.)

Date_____

_____
Church person doing reference check

C. Step #3: The questioning.

Once the reference receives the waiver or otherwise agrees to speak with you, proceed with the questioning as listed below, but be prepared for negative responses. It would be wonderful to obtain responses on each and every question, but the reference may be unwilling to take the time, may have a work policy against sharing such information, or may simply refuse to do so. Again, be as thorough as possible in documenting both responses and non-responses.

The first category of questions, verifying information found on the job application, is the easiest to address. It will be most convenient to keep the application handy for this section. As the questions are asked, the information given by the reference will be compared with that on the application, and then a check mark will be placed on the Reference Check Form if the answers are compatible. If information given by the reference differs from that on the application, it can be noted more fully on the lines following that question. (See Reference Check Form, Appendix.) The following information, at a minimum, should be verified:

<u>Application Verification Questions</u>:
- What was the employee's title?
- What were his/her major responsibilities?
- Were you his/her immediate supervisor?
- If not, who was?
- What was his/her start and end date?
- What was his/her start and end salary ?
- Is he/she eligible for re-hire?
- For what reason did he/she leave your employment?
- How many absences did he/she have last year? (If exact information is not available, was absenteeism a problem?)
- How many days was he/she tardy? (Again, if no information is available, was tardiness a problem?)

The second set of questions covers the skills and abilities of the applicant as they pertain to the position applied for. Again, this section should have been customized before the start of the reference check, in order to add or delete more particular questions.

This section should be easier to move into once the reference has been "warmed up" by verifying the purely factual information above. Begin by defining for the reference the position the applicant is applying for (reading the job description may be helpful), including such factors as the statements of faith or moral obligation. The information should reveal to the former employer as much as possible about the position and the type of person being sought to fill it. Such inclusive information may prompt additional thoughts. Following is a list of generally applicable questions.

Applicant's Fitness for this Position:

- Does this applicant have the skills required by this position?
- In your estimation, does this applicant have the personality and disposition required in this position?
- Would you feel comfortable placing this applicant in this position?
- Are there any reasons why you might hesitate to place the applicant in this position, were you the one doing the hiring for it?
- Without listing particular details, do you feel we should continue our search for a more suitable applicant for this position?
- From what you know of this person, would you have any reservations about his employment in a church ministry?

The final list of questions is furthest from being purely factual and job skill oriented, but relates instead to the applicant's personal characteristics. These may be some of the most revealing if you can get responses to them. They should be asked following the above questions, but chances are that if the reference is unwilling to address the prior questions, these will certainly be left untouched.

Personal Characteristics:

- How well did this person relate and work with others?
- Did you enjoy working with this individual?
- What were this applicant's greatest assets?
- What were this applicant's greatest weaknesses?
- Are there any additional comments you could make that might be helpful to us?

Step #4: Asking for secondary sources.

Before you conclude, ask the reference if there is anyone else that might be able to give additional information. A secondary reference may have a very different opinion of the applicant from that of the first reference, or may know the applicant better personally, resulting in additional personal information. Note this person's name on the Reference Check Form and conduct a reference check with him as well.

Step #5: Concluding the reference check.

In concluding the reference check, thank the reference for his time. If a reference has been particularly helpful, a brief thank-you note may be appropriate and may cultivate a reference's willingness to cooperate again in the future.

Remember, the reference check is vital in screening out potentially harmful or dangerous employees and in helping the church defend itself should any injury later occur. Also, no check will be helpful in defending the church if it has not been documented.

Summary Step #8

It is increasingly essential, and sometimes legally required, to conduct certain background checks on potential employees. In our mobile society where we know less about even church members, a church should establish clear policies and procedures for conducting record checks of applicants whose positions call for special caution, or perhaps of all employees as a matter of routine.

A long-time employee of the church is the chaperon for a youth weekend retreat. Upon their return from the retreat, a parent files suit against the employee and the church as a result of an attempted sexual attack on a youth during the retreat. The church claims it was not negligent in hiring or allowing the employee to chaperon the group, as he had been employed by the church for several years in various church management roles without incident. Could the suit against the church succeed?

If the employee had a criminal history of such abuse and the church had not run a background check, the claim may succeed. A jury could easily find that the church was unreasonable in not running the criminal background check for anyone with this type of access to youth or children. The fact that the employee had no previous incidents within the church is probably irrelevant, since this propensity would not have come to light in his other positions with the church.

I. USE OF RECORD CHECKS

The record checks referred to here include the criminal record check, the driver's license record check, and the credit record check. Each can be a good predictor of certain types of behavior, and when very harmful behavior can be predicted and harm thus avoided, the record checks become worth their weight in gold to the employer.

Many employers hesitate to use these checks for a number of reasons:

- First, they generally hire by word of mouth or from within the congregation, and feel the check is either unnecessary (since they know the individual) or insulting to the applicant, or both.

- Second, they don't know the logistics of running a record check and therefore may find it intimidating or inconvenient to learn to do so.

- Third, since the church may not realize the frequency and magnitude of abuse incurred by victims of "long-time church employees" and trusted clergy, churches seem to think such things can only happen somewhere else and thus don't protect against them.

- Fourth, the church or employer does not understand the enormous legal risk being taken by failing to do an appropriate check--negligent hiring cases continue to arise based on such inaction.

Keep in mind that in a negligent hiring suit, the jury will be assessing the "reasonableness" of the employer's (church's) actions in discovering information about an applicant that could have been used to prevent a later harm. If an applicant has a criminal record of sexual assault and a church hires the applicant to supervise the day-care center without running a criminal record check, the church will have a very hard time defending its actions should an incident arise. The jury could easily find that the record check would have been simple and inexpensive to run, the potential (and actual) harm was great, and the church was "unreasonable" in not taking this small step to avoid a great danger. In other words, the church would be guilty.

Because of the enormity of the harm, the damage to the reputation and trust within the church, congregation, and community, and the extensive monetary losses involved in a legal suit, churches must take a careful look at their hiring guidelines. Given the gravity of the situation, blind faith in fellow parishioners is no longer enough. The staff and all applicants need to be educated on such dangers, and regular record checking procedures implemented for *all* applicants. Applicants will not be offended if it is standard policy for everyone. In fact, they should feel that it is their duty to do their part in protecting members from harm and in setting up programs which will display concern and demonstrate active recognition and prevention of such harm.

The key to using record checks effectively is to recognize when you *must* check a record, when it would be *advisable*, and when it might be highly *invasive of a person's privacy* or plain discriminatory to do so. There are very few times when a record check is legally required to be run, but since the jury will always be looking at the employer's reasonableness in running (or not running) a check, the employer must make an informed decision in deciding whether or not to do so.

One final note—volunteers, as well as employees, are considered agents of the employer (church), and the employer will be held to the same standard of care in bringing a volunteer on board as it would be for an employee. So, consider each of the record checks with the volunteer in mind as well--it may be imperative to run the checks on some volunteer employees.

II. WHEN AND HOW TO RUN A CRIMINAL RECORD CHECK

The criminal record check is *required* by some states when applicants are being hired to work in daycares, including church daycares. Each state has a different procedure for running a check, and various departments in each state handle this activity. One or two phone calls is all it takes to determine the process in your state. Simply call the local sheriff's department or magistrate's office and inquire--they will point you in the right direction.

North Carolina has a statute providing that persons convicted of child neglect, abuse, moral turpitude, or users of illegal drugs or excessive alcohol may not be child-care workers. (NCGS §110-91). Checking the criminal record of an applicant is an obvious way to assure compliance with this state prohibition. In North Carolina, while checking for a criminal record in a specific county is rather simple, seeking information of a state-wide or national basis, is not at all easy, and in some respects almost impossible officially.

At the county level, the employer submits to officials the full name, maiden name, date of birth, and how many years the employer would like the record check to go back. (All of this information can be found on the I-9 form filled out by the applicant.) In Harnett County, N.C., for example, the information for the request is sent to the Clerk of Court, Criminal Division, along with $5.00 per request. (Note that within North Carolina, counties use either the Sheriff's Department or Magistrate's Office to conduct these checks--call and confirm the process before implementing it in your area.) There is no official form to fill out, so writing the information on regular paper will suffice. Or, it may be easier to access the records by going to the courthouse and requesting the information in person. There will still be a $5.00 fee and a short wait, but most areas will be happy to honor such requests. Another way to get the information is to require the applicant to obtain a copy of the desired records and return them before the interview.

While there is a state-wide data bank, and that information is available at the county level, no present law permits the release of this information to private persons. Thus a private day-care operator, or church cannot lawfully obtain the information even with the consent of the individual whose record is being sought. The same is true with the federal records.

There are now suggestions being made that this information be made available, at least with the consent of the individual whose record is sought, so that employers may obtain the information. Right now, the only practical way to obtain it in North Carolina is to hire an investigator who then probably knows some police officer who can run the search, even though the officer may not legally do so.

The one short-fall in using the county criminal record check is that each county keeps records only for crimes committed in that county. Therefore, it is virtually impossible to run a thorough record check without calling every county in the country.

There is, however, one way to minimize this limitation. The application should obtain information on all past employment and residences. You should note any unexplained gaps where information may have beem omitted. Depending on the nature of the position, you could then pursue a criminal background check in other counties or even states. The procedures for obtaining such information vary, however, from state to state. The Clerk of Court in any county in the United States could provide information on how to check criminal records in that jurisdiction.

Criminal record checks for positions other than in the day care are made at the option of the employer--however, the legal ramifications of not running them when appropriate leave little option. When determining whether or not a criminal record check should be run for various positions or employees, consider a few questions:

- Is there a high risk of harm in this position?
  E.g., is there access to children and youth?
  Is the employee unsupervised much of the time?

- Will this employee potentially move out of the position presently being filled and into a more risky position?

- Would an employee with a criminal record be unsuitable for the position being applied for?

- Does the church have a policy of re-examining qualifications and running new reference checks when old employees move from position to position?

- If you were moving your family to a new congregation, would you want workers in this position to have clear criminal records?

- Would you hesitate to risk a child's safety and stake the reputation and financial security of the church on this applicant's integrity?

If the answer to any of the above questions is "yes", you would be strongly advised to run a record check. The $5.00 charge and time spent on the check will pay off immeasurably should harm be avoided as a result.

III. HOW AND WHEN TO RUN A DRIVER'S LICENSE CHECK

A driver's record check will often be handled by the church's insurer when official "driving" positions are being filled. Anyone the church authorizes to drive the church van, for example, must usually be reported to the insurer, who runs a driving record check before approving the person under the insurance plan, and then thereafter runs periodic checks to keep its records updated.

The more questionable check arises when volunteers or others are "shuttling" youth or employees from place to place frequently, or are otherwise doing a lot of unofficial driving with their private vehicles. A driver's record check is not legally required in these circumstances, but as noted above, the legal ramifications of not running the appropriate check leaves little option for the employer. Again, the employer must proceed carefully if this check is not run.

Some quick questions to use in analyzing the potential for risk and the advisability of running a driver's record check:

- Does this job description require driving?

- Does this job occasionally require driving?

- Is it reasonably foreseeable that this person could be driving others in the regular course of his position?

- If this position does not require driving, is it foreseeable that the person hired for the position could one day move into such a position without his driving record being further checked?

Again, if the answer to any of the above is "yes" and the church fails to run a driver's record check on applicants for the position, a jury could easily consider such actions "unreasonable" and thus find the church guilty of negligent hiring should an accident result.

In most states, driving records are open to the public (as in North Carolina) and can be accessed via a simple request. In North Carolina, a copy of the driver's license can be obtained by the employer through the Department of Motor Vehicles for a $5.00 charge, or the employer could request the applicant obtain the copy and submit it during his interview.

IV. HOW AND WHEN TO RUN A CREDIT CHECK

A. Are Credit Checks Discriminatory?

Unlike the other types of record checks, the credit check has raised some question as to its potentially discriminatory nature. Statistically, persons with credit problems and bankruptcy filings are more often economically disadvantaged, and a higher percentage of these people are from minority classes. Thus, the systematic use of the credit check for all positions being filled often has a disparate impact on the hiring of minorities, and is now considered discriminatory. For this reason, the credit check should be used only when a correlation can be shown between the need for such information and the nature or requirements of the position being filled.

> *Example: A church is going to hire an applicant to handle its payroll and accounting functions and to be responsible for other fiscal decisions. This person will also have access to church funds and control over disbursements. The church eliminates an applicant from consideration when his credit check reveals a poor credit history and a bankruptcy filing. The applicant files a discrimination claim stating that his record results from his being poor and a minority and has nothing to do with his ability to perform the functions of the job. Could he win?*

> *Questionable. Even assuming the church is subject to liability for discrimination of this sort, the church has a responsibility to its members to handle funds and donations carefully, and someone with a record of making poor financial decisions, particularly when the applicant has access to church funds and will handle their disbursement, may logically be a poor choice. Reference checks from other employers, a criminal record check revealing embezzlement, or a history of bad check writing may further substantiate the church's decision, but may not be necessary in order to defend the church's actions.*

B. When Should a Church Routinely Run A Credit Check?

A church should run a credit check on anyone handling finances or making fiscal decisions for the church. It is the church administration's responsibility to oversee the funds the church collects, and it would be clearly negligent on the church's part NOT to check into an applicant's ability or integrity in handling such matters before giving him access to church funds. Using reasonable care and common expectations should result in the church making good decisions as to the requiring of a credit record check for a particular position. But keep in mind that the information is available and is often helpful in selecting good applicants for key positions.

C. How Do You Obtain a Credit Report?

Various private credit reporting agencies provide credit checks, or information can be received in certain circumstances through local banking and credit references. Whichever is utilized, the applicant must be informed ahead of time that the check will be made. In order to document that the applicant was informed of the credit check and consented to it, it may be advisable to have the applicant sign a release. The release could look like this:

Authorization for Release of Credit Information

I hereby authorize the ABC Baptist Church to check my credit history with all appropriate sources. Such information may be obtained for the years _____ to the present.

Applicant Name _____
    Other names applicant has used (maiden name, prior married name)

    _____

Applicant SS #   _____

Driver's License # _____

Bank Names and Account Numbers (during period credit check covers)

    _____

    _____

    _____

                             _____
                              Applicant's Signature and Date

A credit service will generally require the applicant's name, address, social security number (This drives the request.), and driver's license number, along with $30.00 to $40.00 to run the check. It will produce a report of all charge card payment records, judgments, bankruptcy filings, and reports by anyone who has reported a problem collecting payment from the individual.

An employer might also consider asking the applicant for bank and credit references. Banks are generally reluctant to release information on personal accounts, but the potential employer's bank may be willing to request the information from the listed bank. If the information is important enough (a CFO is being hired in a very large church or organization, for example), the banks will probably be happy to cooperate in order to help ensure the financial stability of their clients. The bank reference check will require the bank names and account numbers, and the information produced will include the average account balance, how long the account has been open, and how many NSF checks have been reported.

If the applicant has been employed in prior positions, make certain the prior two employers are contacted. If the applicant is presently employed, negative information may not have surfaced yet within that organization. Supplement this information by contacting the employer before the applicant's present position. This reference's information may be much more complete.

Conclusion

Criminal record, driver's license, and credit checks can provide instant documentation and justification for many hiring decisions. They also verify employment application information and supply information for further discussion with the applicant. Since these checks are mandatory or highly suggested in certain legal contexts, the employer must carefully analyze the potential risks and liabilities in each position, and select and administer checks accordingly.

STEP #9: FINAL HIRING AND REJECTION

Summary Step #9

The hiring group or person is now ready to hire an applicant, and also must notify those not being hired. How this is done is important, not only legally, but in terms of assuring a mutual understanding with the person offered the position, and in relationships with those who are not chosen. The offer, in particular, is a very important document with substantial legal implications, and it should be drafted carefully.

Both offers of employment and rejection letters are important in concluding the actual hiring process, and for separate and distinct reasons, both must be handled carefully.

Rejection letters should be handled sensitively for several reasons:

- The church would like to minimize any hard feelings which may arise, especially if the applicant is a member of the church or has friends in the church.

- The church may have found this applicant to be a very strong candidate for this or other positions and would like to affirm his strengths and encourage him in his job search.

- The church may wish not to close the door to possible future consideration of the applicant for other positions.

- The church wants to minimize the potential for discrimination claims by those not selected for employment.

Offers of employment must also be carefully crafted. Deficiencies in the offer of employment could result in claims of unlawful discharge. Offers of employment must be complete and thorough in order to establish concrete parameters within which the newly employed person will operate and be evaluated. Failing to outline a clear job description and standards for evaluation could inhibit an employer's ability to promptly terminate the employee for failing to meet specified job requirements or expectations.

I. EXTENDING AN OFFER

Once an employee has been selected, it is important to make a complete and well-defined offer. This offer is often made in an "offer" interview, with a follow-up letter noting the same elements. The advantage of an offer interview is that it gives an immediate opportunity to clarify any uncertainties and for the applicant to ask additional questions. The written offer can then reflect the modified understandings or further classifications that developed in the offer interview.

A number of items should be included in the offer, and creating a simple checklist to make sure all are discussed may be advisable. The following items should be routinely discussed:

1. First, the employer should review the job description, Statement of Faith, Statement of Moral Obligation, and statement of rules and policies, with the applicant.

2. Another critical inclusion is the labeling of the position as "at-will" unless the church actually intends the position to be a contractual position of guaranteed longer duration. It is imperative that the "at-will" status of the position be made clear (unless this has been intentionally altered within the employment contract) during the hiring process. Do not make any implications about the employee's position lasting longer than is at the will of either the employer or employee. Further, do not make any inadvertent implications to this effect by labeling the first period of work as "trial" or "temporary." This could be interpreted as implying that the period following the trial or temporary period must then be "permanent," which will negate the "at-will" doctrine. If this period is actually just the time before the employee will be eligible for benefits, address it in that manner.

   The employee handbook can also negate the "at-will" status of a position. If the handbook outlines a termination process, the employer must follow the process and can no longer terminate truly "at-will." Without an employee handbook, an employer can still be deemed to have negated the at-will status through the established practice of giving employees warnings, etc. If the employer generally follows certain practices in terminating employees, even if the practices are purely generous and voluntary, these practices can be construed as an implication that termination will be proceeded by such actions, again negating the "at-will" doctrine and the accompanying ability to terminate a person without cause or prior notice.

3. Salary should also be clearly stated while making the offer. Do not use the term "annual," since this has been held to imply that the employee was hired on an annual contract and is thus due an annual salary. This can result in the employer being held liable for the entire year's salary even though the employee was terminated before the end of that year. Bonuses and other compensation should also be laid out. Provide such information in writing, as well as a disclaimer stating that such a compensation program is subject to change at the discretion of the employer.

4. All policies regarding attendance, dress, or office procedures should be spelled out as well. If the organization has an employee handbook, most such items should be addressed within it. If there is no handbook, try to be as thorough as possible in conveying complete information (placing such items on the checklist would again be helpful). Make sure items that could result in termination (too many absences), rather than just inconvenience (having to figure out how to obtain office supplies), are covered completely.

5. Let the employee know what feedback can be expected, from whom, and when. This should include specifying the areas that will be monitored and upon which he will be evaluated, as well as additional less tangible areas that the employer will be evaluating. If there will be a six-month review, for example, clearly define the time frame as well as the items to be covered at that time. Also, define who will be available to answer questions and to provide feedback between review periods. Make sure the person knows where to go for help should the need arise.

6. Request a written acceptance response, and indicate a deadline for receiving the response. File a copy of your letter of offer as well as the new employee's response in his personnel file.

The key is to relay enough information so that the new employee knows what to expect. If the above areas are covered and the employee's questions addressed, as well as a channel specified through which later arising questions can be answered, the employee should have a good feel for what is expected and what he/she needs to do to perform well in the new position. Err on the side of too much information, not too little. Clarity in all of the above areas establishes consistent expectations and will result in fewer areas of contention--and fewer resulting legal suits.

II. THE EMPLOYEE HANDBOOK

An additional note on the employee handbook. If a handbook is utilized by the church, keep in mind that it may be seen as an extension of the employment contract. In that case all terms, rules, policies, benefits, and, in fact, all contents of the handbook would then become part of the contract--and the employer would be contractually obligated to provide them. If this is not the intention of the employer, clearly and conspicuously state that the handbook is NOT a part of the employment contract, and further, that its contents are subject to change, deletion, or addition at the discretion of the employer. Have this statement signed by the new employee and file it in his personnel file. This should be sufficient in avoiding added responsibilities arising from an innocuous inclusion in the employee handbook.

Example:

"I have read and understand the contents of this employee handbook. I understand that the employee handbook is an expression of current policy and may be altered at any time at the sole discretion of my employer. I further understand that no statements or implications contained in the employee handbook will be read to constitute an extension of my employment contract, and will in no way affect the status of my "at-will" employment."

_____   _____
Employee Signature   *Date*

III. WRITING A REJECTION LETTER

If an applicant is not chosen, it is generally advisable to inform him promptly. While this can be uncomfortable for some people, it is probably the only way to eliminate inquiring phone calls. In reality, some applicants may be excluded from further consideration rather early in the process, while others are still viable candidates late in the process. Indeed, if there are several acceptable candidates, the church may not wish to reject other acceptable candidates until the preferred applicant has formally accepted the position.

No rejection letter or call is required by law, and should a rejection letter be sent, no explanation regarding the employment decision is required by law, either. Therefore, the employer has some latitude in this area.

First, the most careful and preferred route is to create a form letter containing as little specific information as possible. The fact that the employer has selected another applicant, along with a pleasant appreciation of the applicant's interest in the position, is sufficient. If the employer feels the unchosen candidate was very well qualified (though not as qualified as the one chosen) or for some particular reason deserves an explanation, the employer may choose another course.

The second option is to give feedback on why the applicant was not hired. If this option is chosen, make certain the explanation clearly reflects that the selection was based on all applicants' abilities to perform essential functions of the job. If any other explanation is offered or enters the conversation, a legal suit could follow.

> *Example: The church finally chooses between two very qualified candidates for a financial manager position. When the pastor relays the decision to the unchosen applicant, the applicant is very hurt and requests a reason for the decision. The pastor, trying to be compassionate, relays that the applicant, a female, was indeed very qualified, but all things being equal, they had decided to hire a male because the parishioners and staff were used to having a male in the position and they didn't know if they would accept the decisions or authority of a female. The applicant sues for sex discrimination. Could she win?*
>
> *Probably, and the church blatantly set itself up for a sexual discrimination suit by relaying such information to the candidate. The pastor's own words that the decision was made based on gender will be difficult proof to overcome in a court of law.*

Since those in authority never know exactly what information might be relayed to a rejected applicant by a well-intentioned employee, a standard policy of utilizing form letters without additional details is a good practice. Any embellishment could be trouble.

Summary Step #10

Whew! Almost done. But there are some wrapping up things to do. Chief among these is the creating of a file of all the key materials that you have used during the process. There are also other records of your employment process which should be retained, at least for a while, in case questions should arise.

We have stressed the importance of a standardized employment system and good documentation throughout this text. However, once the system is in place and all relevant information is documented and filed, what happens next? The documents must then be retained properly as well.

Keep in mind that if the church were to be sued for negligent hiring or discrimination, retained documents would be the church's proof that it acted reasonably and legally in making employment decisions. (They would also support the church's proper actions regarding payment of employment taxes, necessary employee safety training, and other employment matters.) Therefore, it is critical that the church be able to access such information should the need arise.

The federal government, and sometimes the state government as well, requires that certain types of documents be retained for a set period of time. This ensures that all relevant evidence will be available should a question or lawsuit arise. If the church has not retained such records, a court may assume that the claim being made is valid. The church would then lose its case since it would not have the required documentation to refute the claim being made. Additionally, the errant employer may also be fined.

Different laws may also address the same records. For example, the Age Discrimination and Employment Act requires that applications be kept for one year. However, the Civil Rights Act allows discrimination suits to be brought for six years after the alleged discrimination occurred. To be truly protected, then, many employers choose to keep such information for the full six-year period.

If more than one regulation requires a retention period for the same set of documents, the employer must keep the records for the longest of these periods. This occurs frequently with payroll and tax requirements pertaining to employee records.

Some federal guidelines merely stipulate that the records be kept for a "reasonable" amount of time. Though "reasonable" has not been statutorily defined in this sense, the courts have determined "reasonable" to mean three years unless circumstances exist which would require reasonable employers to retain them longer. This means that if such records are disposed of after three years, the court will presume that the employer acted reasonably unless the opposing party can establish otherwise.

All records are handled differently. Some types of records are required to be kept for a relatively short period of time, while an employer would normally keep them longer for purposes such as tracking employment, retention, or training trends. In these cases, the employer will actually choose to retain records longer than required by law.

In other cases, the employer will have no use for such records and will keep them only to meet the legal retention requirements. These records are basically "taking up space," and need to be handled differently than those with their own intrinsic value. They should be systematically destroyed as soon as the retention period expires.

Although there are retention requirements for many types of records, and many laws overlap, following is a concise list of those relevant to the hiring processes addressed in this text. Most personnel record requirements are controlled by federal law, so only federal law is outlined below.

- The Age Discrimination in Employment Act (ADA) requires applications, resumes, advertising, and other pre-employment records to be kept for one year (90 days for temporary positions). Even applications of those hired need only be kept under this Act for one year.

- The Occupational Safety and Health Administration requires that medical records (not including health insurance claims) be retained for the term of employment plus thirty years.

- The Civil Rights Act has a six-year statute of limitations, so many employers retain detailed records of employee actions for this length of time, even though other acts (like the ADA) only require that records of personnel actions to be kept for one year from the date of the action.

- Active employee files must be kept for three years.

- Terminated employee files must be kept for one year.

There are also retention requirements for payroll records, pension plans, promotions, training, termination procedures, and even any exposures to hazardous substances, but these are beyond the scope of this text. A more complete discussion of all record-keeping requirements may be found in "Record Keeping Requirements" and "Records Retention Procedures: Your Guide to Determine How Long to Keep Your Records and How to Safely Destroy Them!". Both are written by Donald Skupsky and published by the Information Requirements Clearinghouse, Denver, CO.

So what should the church do?

A simple schedule can be developed to help organize your file retention procedures. Since the law is sometimes difficult to pin down (e.g., when it requires retention for a "reasonable" time), and since some churches or organizations utilize employment records for other purposes (e.g., tracking retention), each organization should examine its own record-keeping needs and decide on an appropriate retention schedule. Your attorney should approve any plan before it is implemented.

To stay within the scope of this text, following is a retention schedule that would go a long way in establishing a proper schedule for the documents covered here. Keep in mind, however, that there are good reasons to keep records longer than the *legally required* time listed here (e.g., documentation for legal defense, administrative record keeping, tracking of trends, etc.). An attorney's advice may be invaluable here.

- Job description, Statement of Faith, Statement of Moral Obligation, Church Rules and Policies, Employment Manual (if applicable): the last year of its use + 10 years

- Copy of any advertising or recruiting pieces: 1 year

- Application form for those applicants then hired: 3 years

- Application form for those applicants then rejected: 1 year

- I-9 form: 3 years from date of hire OR 1 year from date of termination, whichever is later

- All hiring records, including the Reference Release forms (copies of those signed and sent), Reference Checking forms, Criminal Record Release form (if applicable), Criminal Record, (The Employment Checklist and Rejection Letter might also be considered hiring records.): 1 year

- Interview Worksheet and any supplements: 1 year

- Copy of the driver's record, driving tests, and education records: 3 years

- Testing records: 1 year

- Medical exams or records: current year + 5 years

- Employee files: 3 years

- Employment contracts: the last year of its use + 6 years

In additional consideration in the proper filing and retention of the records listed above is the confidentiality of such records. No personal information should ever be available to employees other than those with a "need to know". Taking great care to share such information within the organization on a "need to know" basis will ensure that confidentiality and the applicant's right to privacy are upheld.

In a related concern, the employer may not want an employee to have access, once hired, to the reference check responses, etc., acquired during the hiring process. This is an interesting dilemma, since employees have a legal right to view their employment files. If there is information you would not want shared, make certain you will not need such information to establish a legal defense at some point in the future, and then eliminate such information from the files. Of course, if the law requires retention of such information, there is no way to keep it from being viewed by the employee.

Obviously, files containing personal data should be kept in a secure, locked place. Again, only those with a need to know should have access to such files.

POSTSCRIPT: ASSURING A THOROUGH PROCESS SUCH AS THIS

When a church is called to defend itself in an employment-related lawsuit, one of its most convincing and waterproof arguments will be that it established fair and effective employment procedures, followed them consistently, and documented everything along the way. The simplest way to achieve this is to prepare an "employment packet" before hand. The packet should include all of the necessary forms and worksheets and a checklist the church can use to double check its thoroughness. The packets should then be used in hiring for any position within the church.

If a lawsuit proceeds to trial, the jury will be judging the church on the "reasonableness" of its actions. The more "ammunition" the church has, the more effort it appears to have made to safeguard others from harm; and the more established and uniform its use of these safeguards, the more likely the jury will find for the church.

I. THE EMPLOYMENT PACKET

The employment packet is partly a matter of convenience for the employer and partly a method for avoiding legal problems. An employment packet should contain each of the pieces required by the employment system so that it is quickly and easily reached and utilized when needed. Having the information already compiled also reduces the risk that a form will be missed or that a step will be skipped when it becomes time to interview an applicant--the skipped form may be the one that makes the difference between winning and losing a case. Create and compile the following forms into ready-made packets. (Having the interview sheet or application printed as a fold-out sheet will provide a quick and convenient holder).

- Employment packet checklist
- Copy of the church's Statement of Faith
- Copy of the church's rules and policies
- Copy of the Statement of Moral Obligation, if applicable
- Application
- I-9 form
- Release forms for reference check (at least 3)
- Reference check form to help perform effective reference checks and to provide uniform documentation of responses
- Release form for driving record check (not required in North Carolina)
- Release form for criminal record check (not required in North Carolina)
- Release form for credit report
- Interview sheet
- Supplemental interview sheet for overflow

II. THE CHECKLIST

The checklist is a simple mechanism used to guarantee that the system is properly implemented. It is particularly useful if different people will be handling various stages of the process, or if more than one decision-maker is involved, since each can quickly determine what steps remain to be completed, and a simple final check can be made before the file is closed. This form will be updated as the applicant proceeds through the employment process, and will ultimately be returned to the file as a verification that all steps have been completed.

The checklist can also be used as a "road map" through the process, as the order that certain steps are performed in is often critical. All of the forms listed before the "interview conducted" line should be completed and filed before the interview. After the interview, the interview worksheet and any additional relevant information (for example, a resume) will be placed in the packet, and the reference gathering stage will begin. After performing the record and reference checks, return the results to the folder. As the various steps are completed, the information should be added to the packet and the checklist updated accordingly. Once the applicant has been accepted or rejected, the file will be complete and available for future reference and documentation, should the need arise.

EMPLOYMENT CHECKLIST

_____ Application completed; file created

_____ I-9 completed for employees (not required for volunteers); filed separately

_____ Reference release forms filled out and signed; copies made (one sent to reference, one kept in file)

_____ Job description presented and signed; filed

_____ Statement of Faith presented; signed by applicant; returned to folder (not required for volunteers)

_____ Statement of Moral Obligation presented, signed by applicant; returned to folder (not required for volunteers)

_____ Church Rules and Policies presented; signed by applicant; returned to folder

_____ Interview conducted:

> Interviewer: _____
> Date: _____

_____ Criminal record checked in the following states; results filed: (mandatory for child care "employees")

> _____ _____
> _____ _____

_____ Driver's record checked; results filed

_____ Credit record checked; results filed (for clergy and positions with a direct correlation to such records)

_____ Signed reference release forms sent to references

_____ References contacted; reference check forms completed; filed

_____ Drug test run; results filed

_____ Rejection letter sent; copy filed

_____ Offer made to applicant; date: _____

_____ Medical record checked (post-offer only); results filed

_____ Acceptance letter sent; copy filed

Section C: Special Hiring Contexts

1. Clergy

2. Child Care

3. Volunteers

4. A Note on Independent Contractors

CONSIDER THESE CASES:

- A state supreme court has held a denomination liable for punitive damages of 12 million dollars because it had been grossly negligent in not acting to prevent the persistent sexual abuse of children by a pastor.

- In a southern state, a Baptist church and former pastor has been sued by a member and her spouse alleging the pastor abused his counseling relationship with the woman by engaging in sexual relations with her; and that the church was negligent in hiring the pastor because of evidence of prior ethical misconduct and in failing to properly supervise his counseling. The church was unaware of the misconduct, but the suit alleges the church should have known and would have if it had properly monitored his conduct.

- In California, a prominent church and pastor were sued for clergy malpractice when a counselee committed suicide.

Increasingly, churches and the clergy are being sued for misconduct. Clergy today are increasingly subject to suits for clergy malpractice, infliction of emotional distress, counseling malpractice, defamation, and a host of other imaginative legal claims. These sometimes arise out of quite proper clergy ministries of counseling and preaching, but, sadly, also often arise because of clear misconduct including sexual misconduct toward parishioners, counselees and others. National attention has also been drawn to instances of repeated sexual misconduct toward children.

These lawsuits and the awards given by juries to plaintiffs make clear that despite the high office of pastor, the ethical presumptions of those who aspire to the office, and the spiritual commitments professed by such persons, the pastors are not immune from the temptations common to mankind and the pressures of contemporary culture.

Churches find themselves involved in these lawsuits as well. Plaintiffs, as we noted in Chapter 1, frequently allege the church is liable for this misconduct either on the theory of *respondeat superior* or on a claim that the church was negligent in the hiring and/or supervision of the pastor.

Of course, the potential legal damage from such misconduct is probably minor compared to the spiritual damage to the church and its ministry. But certainly the legal aspects reinforce what ought to be a central concern for churches — taking all reasonable steps to assure that the persons whom we call as pastors are spiritually and morally gifted for ministry.

THE PROBLEM:

How can a church, to the greatest extent possible, assure itself of the fitness for ministry of those candidates it considers? What steps can a church take to minimize the risks not only of potential legal liabilities, but also insure the best possibility of calling a person who can minister effectively given the uniqueness of the church's needs and nature?

I. SPECIAL NATURE OF CLERGY ROLE

A. The Spiritual Nature of the Role

There is a uniquely *spiritual* relationship between the church and its clergy. The church and its clergy are one in faith, and work together to study, celebrate, and spread the church's religious faith and doctrines. So entwined are the church and its clergy that it is hard to ascertain when the church or practice of religion ends and where the individual pastor and his/her personal needs and rights begin.

The "calling" of a pastor to a church is an event which involves not only careful human judgment, but also a process which involves spiritual discernment and judgments beyond forms and "steps." In many respects, it is an intensely communal decision, with more parallels to a marriage decision than to a secular factory context. The "match" of gifts, style, and spiritual resonance is for many more important than formal educational qualifications and an array of glorious reference letters.

We do not by any suggestions made here seek to diminish the priority of these spiritual elements. We do suggest, however, that spiritual judgments and discernment are often enhanced by a thorough process of recruitment and assessment. Too often churches may leap too quickly to call a pastor where there is some initial resonance and comfort, but where further inquiry and careful review would have alerted the church to issues and concerns that at a minimum warranted more clarification.

B. Minimal Legal Scrutiny Because of Special Nature of Clergy

This special relationship between the church and its clergy has been recognized by legislatures and courts which have systematically taken a "hands off" approach to any intrusion into this relationship.

Our founding fathers recognized that some aspects of the church were *spiritual*, rather than *tangible* and controllable by secular law. They protected the practice of religion from government intervention in the Establishment Clause of the U. S. Constitution. They realized that when a court, law, or statute attempts to regulate the *spiritual* aspects of the church, such as the clergy-church relationship and the selection of clergy, it comes dangerously close to infringing upon the freedom of religion. Government regulation would inevitably infringe upon the church's ability to lead its congregation to worship, grow, and practice its faith.

As a matter both of constitutional law and legislative policy, neither the courts nor other branches of government have felt themselves either competent or empowered to interfere in the employment decisions regarding clergy. The result is that no hiring situation is more free of regulation than is the decision of a church in employing members of the clergy.

Presently, the *spiritual* decisions made by the church are protected from regulation and review by the courts. A court's attempt to review a church's pastoral selection, for example, would force the court to decide if a hiring decision had been made based on *spiritual* or discriminatory factors. The court is not prepared to "second guess" the spiritual needs and best interests of the church and congregation.

C. Clergy Hiring Not Without Legal Implications

While legislatures do not regulate clergy hiring, this does not mean that there are no legal implications when churches hire clergy. The law still hovers around the relationship to some extent. In each of the following areas, there are legal implications:

1. Negligent Hiring

A church may still be liable if it acts unreasonably in hiring a clergyperson who harms others. Thus, for example, the hiring of a clergyman whom the church knew had a history of child abuse, and which then placed him in an unsupervised situation with children whom he abused might well be liable under a theory of negligent hiring.

2. Liability under Theories of Agency

As we noted earlier, an employer is liable for the harms caused by an employee when those acts are in furtherance of the employer's interests. Thus, a church may sometimes become liable for pastor's negligence.

3. Contract Breach

While courts will not interfere in any matter involving doctrinal or theological questions, they will often enforce rights arising from contracts. Thus, commitments made to a pastor in an employment agreement may be enforceable in a court.

4. Non-religious Employment/tax Law

There is a wide range of laws which govern employer/employee relations which are applicable, and the clergy are not automatically exempt. Tax and reporting laws governing, for example, income tax withholding and social security, cover all employees as do immigration laws.

As a general rule, if the issues can be resolved on the basis of "neutral principles of law" without the necessity of inquiry into theology or matters of internal church governance implicating doctrinal matters, then courts may become involved. If the issue can be separated, analyzed from a clearly legal perspective, and resolved without a spiritual basis or understanding, chances are that the court will be willing to resolve such disputes, and that government will be more likely to regulate these areas in the future.

D. Need for a More Thorough Hiring Process in Calling of Pastoral Staff

Wide publicity has been given in recent years to instances of serious clergy misconduct, including special media attention to clergy misconduct. It does appear that problems of this sort are much more widespread than in previous generations. Not a few leading churches have had to go through painful processes of dealing with clergy involved in serious breaches of personal and professional ethics and conduct clearly inconsistent with their Christian commitment.

Nevertheless, it is a testimony to the broad general integrity of the clergy that despite these highly publicized instances, and the very casual hiring process for clergy, there are relatively few problems.

Baptist leaders are also aware of what appears to be increasing tension in churches over pastoral leadership and not a few serious conflicts in churches between the congregation and the pastor over issues of theology, styles of leadership, and visions of the church as well as the ever-present personality factors.

The misconduct stories and the growing conflicts both have contributed to a greater awareness of the need for a more thorough and effective process of inquiry into the selection of clergy, and especially the need to go beyond the formalities of a few references and a trial sermon. This traditional system seems to increasing numbers of lay people and pastors alike as quite inadequate not simply from any legal perspective, but inadequate for the effective discernment requisite for a pastoral call.

II. SPECIAL HIRING CONCERNS FOR THE PURPOSES OF THIS GUIDE

There are many resources available to assist churches in establishing an effective hiring process. State and regional church leadership are available to assist churches in developing a spiritually and administratively sound process. It is not the purpose of this volume to seek to duplicate or collate their suggestions. There are, however, special concerns related to the hiring process that we believe are too often given inadequate attention and where churches have lacked adequate awareness of guidelines.

Briefly, these areas include the following:

1. Inadequate identification of references.
2. Failure to ask critical questions of references.
3. Too narrow a perspective of requisite skills, gifts and qualities.
4. A far too abbreviated process.

NOTE: MORE THAN CAREFUL HIRING

This Guide focuses on HIRING issues and this chapter on CLERGY HIRING. However, the questions which relate to pastoral leadership and liabilities involve far more than just hiring. Baptist local church governance often gives almost no attention to post-hiring accountability of the pastor. The pastor often is left totally alone—to the detriment of his own spiritual growth and need for community and accountability, and to the detriment of the church. This problem is often enhanced by the fact that in most Baptist contexts, many pastors have very little experience of mutual accoutability in ministry. Many never serve as associates. Many wish to quickly "have their own church." In immature persons, this easily becomes an escape from responsibility—a private kingdom.

It seems to us that a biblical model, while acknowledging the special tasks of a pastor, does not view that role in isolation from the church community and the fullness of gifts in the church; and it certainly does not envisage a pastor without the discipline and care of the church.

While the deacons in many churches may, in some theories, play a nurturing and discipling role with the pastor, in fact, this rarely happens. Some Baptist churches have created a Pastoral Relations Committee whose task is to interface with the Pastor and the congregation on church concerns. Whatever the mechanisms, it is clear that churches need to take more seriously the collegiality of ministry and accountability, and develop mechanisms for such review.

Ministers themselves need to develop accountability structures. Some do this through their local church; others, by identifying fellow pastors with whom they can develop a caring and open, mutual discipling.

III. ELEMENTS OF A SEARCH-RECRUITMENT-CALL PROCESS

The following summary reflects what we believe should be the dimensions of a healthy process for a church in the process of seeking a pastor. Again, we commend churches to consult with their Director of Missions, State Convention, and the many materials available from them and others in framing this process.

A. Committing the Church to a Healthy, Thorough Process

This involves the church, at the outset, recognizing the need for a careful, thorough process, and will include:

1. Selection of Skilled Interim Leadership (both lay and pastoral)
2. Identification, Tasks, and Processes of a Search Committee
3. Dealing with Transition Dynamics
4. Assuring the Support of the Whole Church
5. Recognizing Where to Get Help

B. Self-Assessment of the Nature and Needs of the Church and Its Ministry

It is essential that the church know itself before it seeks pastoral leadership. While some aspects of its identity will be self-evident and conscious to the membership, other dimensions may be more subtle, or even ignored. Various instruments have been developed by church leadership to help churches assess their identity, needs and mission. The use of such instruments as part of a whole-church process can be a very healthy contribution to self-understanding of strengths and commitments on the one hand, and needs and weaknesses on the other.

Among the questions such instruments commonly help a church examine are these:

What is the church's personality? history?
Where is the church now in its ministry?
What changes are taking place in the life of the church—
     e.g. demographics, leadership, styles?
What is the history of the church's dealings with, and expectations of, pastors?
How are decisions made in the church?

Where does the church need growth? help?
What are deepest abiding convictions of the church which shape its identity?
What is the church's place in the community? How do others perceive us?
How do we relate to other churches, world missions, community needs?
Church financial resources and other "terms of employment"

C. Identification of Qualities, Gifts, Skills, and Styles of Appropriate Pastor

Unless a church simply wants to find someone "available" who will be a "good ol' boy" and not cause a "problem", churches will need to very carefully identify what it is they are seeking. While such a list may initially suggest a super-human, non-existent being, the prioritization of attributes will help the church assess candidates and candidates assess churches.

Again, there are instruments available to churches in this area which help them look at factors such as the following:

Theological expectations
Ministry style questions
Handling conflict
Specific gifting needs (e.g., if church has major building campaign underway, is starting a private school etc.)
Clergy role issues: prophet, pastor, teacher, administrator, counselor, community leader
Minimal educational/certification issues: ordination, education, training, experience
Marital status expectations or preferences

D. Implementing an Effective Process for Identifying Potential Candidates

Too often churches, even if they engage in an effective process of self-analysis and developing a profile for a candidate, do not give sufficient attention to a broad-based process for identifying potential candidates. Some do little more than accumulate recommendations from personal acquaintances or get a batch of resumes from a Director of Missions or Seminary. While these are among the appropriate means, they should not be the end of the process.

In business contexts, an effective executive search not only considers persons who are presently looking for a job, but attempts to identify names of persons who may be quite satisfied where they are but would be potential ideal candidates.

Churches should engage in an actual "search" as opposed to merely "snaring" a candidate who is passing by. In fact, while many persons may be engaged in a job search who would be quite appropriate, it might be best to seek a candidate who is NOT searching.

Some suggestions to broaden the pool:
Writing to known effective pastors and asking for recommendations
Do not limit the searcg to persons within the state

E. Implement an Initial Screening Process to Reduce the Pool

Churches typically receive many inquiries, and an effective search process should multiply that further. The church needs a process which will quickly filter out those who are not appropriate without engaging in extensive and expensive interviews and personal contacts. The development of a response form to inquiries and candidates may facilitate this process. This response would typically contain two things which will together create a substantial filter:

> First, information about the church—its size, budget, ministry, goals, history etc. A carefully crafted "job description" reflecting the priorities of the church may be appropriate here.

> Second, some preliminary questions about the candidate/applicant. Some churches will utilize a formal job application form, though perhaps a different name would be appropriate. This application should reflect not only obvious questions about education, work history, etc., but should also be tailored to reflect the specific concerns and interests of the church. A well crafted job application will include specific questions, but also some open ended inquiries which enable the candidate to articulate his own sense of ministry, faith and calling. Often, you can learn more from what a person says in an open-ended inquiry than from objective answers to specific questions.

Neither of these initial two documents—job description and application—needs be the full-scale documents which the church may have produced for intensive interviewing, but rather summaries and key questions that are more objective in character—key filtering issues. For example, if a church has a requirement of a seminary degree, or a certain number of years of experience, questions about these factors may quickly reduce the pool.

F. Implementing Comprehensive Screening for Survivors—Serious Candidates

If the initial screening stage has worked well, the pool will be substantially reduced; though there are still likely to be several or even many candidates. At this point, additional processes of screening will be undertaken—perhaps in different stages. The goal is now to narrow the pool substantially to a very few persons.

The types of tools used in this process will be varied:
> Questionnaires—specific and open ended
> Submission of documents from candidates
> Reference checks—church members, denominational leaders, colleagues, community leaders
> Background checks—criminal and credit histories
> Interviews
> Listening to sermons
> Personality testing

We will discuss below the importance and methodology for certain of these items, especially the reference and background checks.

G. "Dating"—Exploring the Relationship with Final Candidates

At some point, most churches will at least temporarily reduce the pool to one principal candidate and pursue that to a conclusion—either their call or elimination at some stage. When the pool is reduced to one person varies among churches. Some would continue through this "dating" stage with perhaps a few "finalists."

The purpose of this stage is, as our name "dating" implies, to explore a little more fully the candidate and how he relates to the church. Too often in Baptist practice, the committee has had a few sessions with the candidate, but the church members know only the factual date on a summary resume and what they hear in a "trail sermon." Even the committee may have had only as few hours with a candidate.

We believe the relationship is so critical and the commitments to one another so serious, that, as we have suggested, it is something like a marriage. It should not be entered into without a significant opportunity to become well acquainted. Search committees should develop means by which they can "see" the candidate and his family in more "real life" situations, rather than simply in formal question and answer discussions.

One mission group always involves candidates for summer missions in a volley ball game. The purpose is to see how they related to a group, a team. Do they dominate the game? Do they respect and include others? Does their personality change in a competitive situation?

While we do not necessarily recommend the volleyball model, it suggests the value of more informal, social contacts in assessing styles and personalities which will have such a major impact.

H. Presenting the Candidate

We believe one of the serious mistakes many churches make is to limit the "presentation" of the candidate to a trial sermon. This "trial sermon" approach is quite inadequate for several reasons:

1. As many ministers have noted, almost everybody has at least one good sermon—it is not a good measure of anything, including preaching ability.

2. It inappropriately elevates preaching ability as virtually the only factor for the church to weigh.

3. It removes the church from effective decision-making since one Sunday sermon provides no realistic basis for a judgment.

4. It often is frustrating to the candidate and his family, who would like a broader basis for interacting with the church members

We suggest a much more broadly based exposure, including meetings with key leadership, informal member groupings, open forums, and, finally, the participation in worship and preaching.

I. Entering Into an Employment Agreement

Churches typically do not enter into binding formal contracts. There are good reasons for this reluctance to enter into any long term binding commitments. However, it is usually necessary to have some formal agreements — salary being only the most obvious. Misunderstanding and hard feelings can often best be avoided by formalizing at least the basic employment terms in some written memorandum such as in a letter from the church to the candidate. It may be important to cover these matters in the final stages of the candidate process. Among the financial and related items that should be covered are:

> Salary
> Benefits (life insurance, medical insurance)
> Retirement contributions beyond salary
> Expenses to be reimbursed (travel, books, continuing education)
> Expense allowances (e.g., state or national convention)
> Housing (Is it furnished?, allowances, utilities, etc.)
> Moving expense allowances
> Vacation days
> Prolonged illness policy

J. Wrapping Up

After the vote and celebration, there are those inevitable formalities which must be observed. Certainly among them will be the creation of file documenting the Search Committees processes and including the evaluations and questionnaires which were part of its search process. These should be retained, at least for the candidate called. Because the files may contain sensitive information, it may be best for the Search Committee Chairman to review the file contents to see if there is anything there which should not be in a file available to the pastor, and, if so, to retain the file outside the church office.

IV. SOME SPECIFIC SUGGESTIONS IN CRITICAL AREAS

A. Asking Probing Questions

Churches probably assume too much. We have seen instances where there were clearly warning signs in the pastoral candidate's background, but nobody asked specific enough questions either of the candidate or of the references provided and churches previously served, so they did not discover vital information. This tendency to superficial inquiry exists at almost every level—theologically, as well as on issues of character, style of ministry and financial integrity.

We do not propose to suggest how the local church ought to probe theological questions, but there are questions which, on issues of background and character affecting legal risks, may help a church discover potential problems. The purpose of such inquiries certainly is not to automatically disqualify A candidate because they have had a problem at some point in their life. It is, however to assure full disclosure, and the opportunity for the church to explore areas of concern.

Here's a brief list of questions which ought to be included in either the application or interview process:

1. Have you ever been charged or convicted of any offense other than a traffic violation? Explain the circumstances and dispositions.

2. Please not the traffic violations for which you have been charged or convicted over the past three years.

3. Have you ever been a party to civil lawsuit? If so, please explain.

4. Have you ever filed for bankruptcy?

5. Have you ever been disciplined by any professional, private or public agency?

6. Have you ever been dismissed by vote of the congregation from the employment of any church? If so, explain.

7. Have you ever resigned from any church position or employment in the face of charges of misconduct? Please explain.

8. Have you ever been treated for alcohol or drug abuse?

9. Have you ever been committed, voluntarily or otherwise, to a hospital for psychiatric care?

10. Have you ever been formally charged or convicted of child abuse?

11. Have employees, staff, members or others with whom you worked ever brought charges of sexual harassment against you either before a church body or any civil governmental agency or court?

12. Are you a lawful resident or citizen?

13. Are you currently under continuing medical care for any condition which would impact you ability to carry out the responsibilities of pastor?

14. In what states have you held driver's licenses in the last ten years?

A. Release Forms

The same release forms utilized for other positions may be used for the pastoral applicants as well, however, it may be best to utilize a more specifically tailored form such as one provided in the Appendix.

There has been some concern that other churches or denominational leaders, are unwilling to share relevant information on former employees. Beyond offering the release forms as discussed previously (See Step #4), the church may go one step further and offer to eliminate any documentation from the applicant's file once a decision has been made and a pastor hired. This will erase a paper trail which might later be discovered by the pastor and reflect negatively on the referring church or official.

Of course, it is always preferable to maintain thorough records, so eliminating such documentation should be the exception, not the rule. If it is the only way to obtain needed information, however, you're better off making the concession, gathering the information, considering it, and then throwing it away. You will still be further ahead than not obtaining the information to begin with.

B. Reference Checks

The general suggestions about reference checks described in the previous sections are applicable here as well. Several points, however, are worth emphasis and additional notes.

First, do not rely solely on references provided by the candidate. Identify other references as well, both by asking named references to identify other persons who may know the candidate as well as taking your own initiative. Obvious potential references are others in ministry in the association or same geographic area of ministry, deacons and other officers of former churches, the Director of Missions, and other denominational officers.

Second, do not rely on written recommendations. Call key references, both his own and those you separately identify.

Third, it is crucial to ask the right questions. Do not assume these people will tell you all they know. They may deliberately decline to reveal questions or concerns, or even known detrimental information. You must use some of the approaches mentioned in the prior sections: emphasize that you have a release, and ask specific questions. Among the most crucial in this context might be the following:

Do you have any information which would give you any reservations about this candidate's appropriateness for pastoral ministry?

Have you had any personal experience or heard reports from others who have questioned this candidates integrity, honesty, ethics, or conduct?

Do you know if this person has ever left a job or ministry position because of accusations related to his conduct or beliefs?

Would you positively recommend this person for ministry at our church?

Have you had any reports of sexual misconduct?

Have any questions been raised regarding his personal finances or his handling of church funds?

What is his reputation among his professional colleagues?

Based on your knowledge and his reputation, is his marriage healthy and stable?

Do you know of any conduct of the candidate's family members which would raise any questions about our church's consideration of him for a ministry here?

Do you have any confidential information you are not free to reveal to us concerning his fitness for ministry?

Fourth, the responses to these questions should be recorded as evidence of the reasonable efforts of the church to ascertain the persons fitness for ministry.

See the sample Pastoral Candidate Reference Check Form in the Appendix.

In conducting a reference check on a pastoral candidate, one variation from the standard process may be helpful. It may be wise to inquire (on the application or during the interview) what other churches the applicant has applied to, and with what results. Follow up by contacting those churches in which the applicant was sincerely considered but was not selected. Finding out why other churches have not selected the applicant may be quite enlightening.

C. Background Checks

Not only should a criminal record and driving record be checked for the pastoral candidate, it may also be run on the pastor's spouse. This is particularly important if the pastor's spouse has traditionally been very active in the church and you expect such activity to continue.

The credit reference check is also critical for the pastor as well as for the spouse. Different financial arrangements within marriages are common, and may have resulted in a financial quagmire for one spouse which would not appear from a financial check on the other. This will require that you notify the spouse that the credit check will be run (which you need to document that you have done), so this step should come much later, say just before the offer is made.

The credit check utilized here should include not only the standard check available from professional credit checking companies (See previous materials.), but also a personal credit check of his/her bank references. And, if the pastor had previously held a position in which he handled church funds, make sure to address his/her financial competence in handling such matters when making the former employer reference checks. If the pastor will have access to church funds, it is critical that the credit check be as thorough as possible.

D. Psychological Data and Testing:

One area that requires further attention when hiring clergy (and perhaps other ministerial personnel as well) is the use of psychological tests. Many large firms, and Christian organizations as well, utilize some forms of psychological testing to evaluate candidates for senior positions. For many, this is a matter of routine, but of course if information is developed in the application or interview which reveals a history of emotional or other problems, such concerns may be intensified.

Three sources of psychological evaluation may be utilized. First, an employer may seek from the applicant reports of prior psychological evaluations. Second, the employer may utilize its own psychological tests for assessing the applicant. Third, an employer may refer the candidate to a professional for an interview and then evaluative report.

Where their is evidence of past serious problems, the church should request a copy of any psychological records from all serious applicants. Additional information may be sought in the interview, and, if the church desires to continue considering the applicant further, a copy of his/her psychological records should be obtained (if there are any). Invasion into this private an area should, however, be restricted to those applicants being seriously considered. The easiest method for obtaining psychological records is to require the applicant to request them from the appropriate source and have them sent directly to the church. This will eliminate the need to design and utilize consent forms, while clearly placing the applicant on notice that the requested information will be sought. Further, because the records will be sent directly from the counselor, there will be no question of any information being eliminated or removed.

There is no way to determine if most psychological records exist unless the applicant volunteers the information. Serious illnesses (requiring hospitalization, medication, etc.) which were paid for through insurance may be traceable through the insurer, and will probably also be uncovered when the new employer adds the minister to the church's insurance policy. (The insurer will probably add the employee or will eliminate coverage for "pre-existing" emotional conditions). Since many policies do not cover any general counseling an applicant may have received, a church must rely on the applicant's straightforwardness in supplying such information.

Psychological tests can be run either as a standard written test or through a personal evaluation. There are a number of "personality" tests marketed by professional testing corporations which could provide limited information on the candidate. These are "canned" tests which are usually returned to the company for "grading" and evaluation. Some are scored by the administrator (church) according to provided instructions.

The "canned" psychological tests can provide a basis on which to start a thorough evaluation, but the use of a professional psychologist retained to conduct a thorough evaluation will make the picture more complete. A psychologist will spend individual time with each applicant and can provide significantly more information. Because of the time and cost involved in the use of this type of evaluation, a church should implement it only as a final step in the hiring process. The written test can be used earlier if limited psychological feedback is desired.

Since every church has its own unique character and personality, and its membership has unique qualities and gifts as well, the same minister will not fit equally well with all churches. The intensive one-on-one evaluation of an applicant can go a long way toward uncovering the applicant's personality traits or beliefs which might create conflict within the church's unique make-up. It might also uncover strengths or weaknesses which make that applicant a poor fit in meeting the church's present needs.

Because dissension involving clergy or key personnel can be so destructive to the church, the congregation, and the personnel involved, the use of extensive psychological testing should be standard practice when hiring for these positions. Oftentimes, the dissension the church seeks to avoid is directly related to the personality (authoritative rather than team-oriented, for example) of key personnel, which for some particular reason does not mesh well with the existing staff or membership. Creating a job description which includes the various traits and characteristics the church desires will help identify what type of person the church is looking for. Utilizing the tests will then help determine whether or not the applicant will fit these requirements.

Dangers of Such "Psychological Profiling"

We are not unaware of the danger of such tests and psychological histories. Two in particular are of concern. First, the danger that psychological profiles may tend to favor "balanced" people, and that most biblical heros and giants of the faith — Jeremiah, Paul, Luther, William Carey—might well have "failed" such tests. Their zeal and singlemindedness might well have been seen by a secular counselor or test as neurotic, dangerous, etc. Certainly we don't want to choose ministers based on finding people who are at the middle of the bell curve of some secularist notion of "normalcy." God certainly calls a wide range of pesonality styles to ministry, and doesn't require them to pass some psychologist's profile. Fortunately, there are Christians in the fields of counseling and testing who are sensitive to these questions and who can help assure that this is not a process to weed out those with genuine spiritual passion, or unique gifts and personalities.

Second, there is a danger such tests might create a false assumption that we can call pastors who don't have problems. Such people don't exist. Pastoral candidates, like all others, have strengths and weaknesses. Perhaps the strongest are those who know their weaknesses and seek spiritual counseling to mature. The tremendous ministry of Paul in the first century, or a Chuck Colson in ours, suggests that God uses not those with no problems and failings, but those who have found the grace of God and let His spirit change their lives. It would be tragic if any review of a counseling and psychological history had the effect of penalizing those who seek the counsel of others to grow and mature in their personal and spiritual life and rewarded those who were blind to their weaknesses or who were unwilling to face up to them.

V. A PARTIAL ILLUSTRATIVE CHURCH PROCESS

What follows is a set of selected materials which were utilized by one church in its pastoral search process. These examples are not intended as a model to be duplicated by other churches, but rather an illustration of ways in which a church may seek to explore areas which are critical to its identity and priorities. Furthermore, since these materials focus almost exclusively on some limited aspects of church assessment and quality priorities, they only cover a small part of the spectrum of a thorough process. Churches should review the materials available from the State Convention and other items noted in the text and bibliography for other illustrations of documents and processes.

(This "Congregational Questionnaire" was developed by the Pastor Search Committee as an attempt to develop a church profile. It focuses on two elements: Part I: Member Profile, and Part II: Priorities for Pastoral Candidate.)

A Church Survey

The Pastor Search Committee is seeking information to determine the general characteristics of our congregation and to provide information about us to candidates for the position. Please help us by answering the following questions. **Circle the best answer.**

Part I: Member Profile

1. Your age:
   Preschool -- Grades 1-6 -- Grades 7-12 -- College/Undergraduate -- Professional School/Graduate Student -- Adult 19-29 -- Adult 30-49 -- Adult 50-64 -- Adult 65+.

2. Your sex: Male---Female.

3. Your marital status: Single --- Married --- Divorced --- Widowed.

4. Number of dependents: 1 2 3 4 5 6 7 8 9 10

5. Educational Level:
   Elementary only --- High School --- Associate degree/Technical college ---
   Bible college --- Bachelor's degree --- Master's Degree ---
   terminal academic or professional degree- -- Ph.D. or other doctoral degree.

6. Distance of your home from the church (in miles): 0-1; 1 - 2; 2 - 5; 5 - 10; 11+

7. How often do you attend Sunday School?
   Weekly --- regularly --- special occasions only --- seldom---not at all.

   How often do you attend Church?
   Weekly --- regularly --- special times only --- seldom --- not at all.

8. For how many years have you been a Christian?
   Less than one --- 1-2 --- 2-5 --- 5-10 --- 10-25 --- longer than 25 .

9. Years a member of _____ First Baptist Church.
   Less than one --- 1-2 --- 2-5 --- 5-10 --- 10-25 --- longer than 25 .

10. Do you give a tithe to _____ First Baptist Church?   Yes --- No.

11. Do you give alms and offerings over and above a tithe, here or elsewhere? Yes---No

12. For how many years have you lived in the vicinity of _____?
    Less than one --- 1-2 --- 2-5 --- 5-10 --- 10-25 --- longer than 25.

13. Are you a native of: _____ --- _____ County --- North Carolina --- Other

14. Do you work?   Full-time --- part-time --- student --- retired --- unemployed.

15. Your occupational category: Graduate student --- clerical --- blue collar ---
    homemaker --- sales --- public school teacher --- college faculty --- college clerical ---
    college staff/administrative --- professional --- special adult --- health care ---
    agricultural ---entreprenuer --- other.

CHURCH SURVEY: PART II. Pastor Profile

Please answer the following questions by circling your preferences
with respect to our new pastor.

1. Must our next pastor be a seminary graduate?   Must---preferred---not important.

2. Must our next pastor have an earned doctoral degree?   Must---preferred---not important.

3. From this list, please rank each characteristic on a scale of 1(not important) to 5 (critical):

_____ a. A man who visits regularly in the homes of members of the congregation.

_____ b. A man who has a vision for ministry to young people.

_____ c. A leader qualified to head financial drives and building programs.

_____ d. A participant in community activities.

_____ e. A man who serves as an example of high moral and ethical character; cultivates
a home and personal life with friends and interests outside local church
activities.

_____ f. A man who dialogues well with individuals about their spiritual development,
religious life, and beliefs; counsels with people facing major decisions of life,
e.g., marriage, major crises, and problems.

_____ g. A man who preaches and teaches the Bible effectively: Biblical principles and
practical guidelines for Christian living.

_____ h. A man who meets the requirements set forth by the Apostle Paul in his letters:
Titus 1:6-9 and 1Timothy 3:1-7.

_____ i. A man able to maintain harmony within the church as it functions on a routine
basis.

_____ j. A participant in denominational activities; able to represent denominational
programs to the congregation.

_____ k. A man who maintains a disciplined program of prayer and personal devotion.

_____ l. A good steward of the financial resources God has given him.

_____ m. A participant in a disciplined program of continuing education.

_____ n. A participant in visitation of new and prospective members.

_____ o. A community leader who is cooperative with social services and charitable
programs.

Pastoral Candidate Profile Survey Results

This is the pastor profile designed by the pastor search committee based on the questionnaire given to the church and on its own prayer and deliberations: (The letter represents the characteristic from the questionnaire. The numbers reflect the priorities given the item first by the church, and second by the Search Committee.)

Group I: The committee and the church agree completely on these traits and characteristics as the first priority for a new pastor. Therefore, the committee concentrated on these to make absolutely certain our recommended pastor has them.

(g)1-1. A man who preaches and teaches the Bible effectively: Biblical principles and practical guidelines for Christian living.

(f)2-2. A man who dialogues well with individuals about their spiritual development, religious life, and beliefs; counsels with people facing major decisions of life, e.g., marriage, and major crises and problems.

(e)3-3. A man who serves as an example of high moral and ethical character; cultivates a home and personal life with friends and interests outside local church activities.

(h)4-4. A man who meets the requirements set forth by the Apostle Paul in his letters: Titus 1:6-9 and 1Timothy 3:1-7.

(k)5-5. A man who maintains a disciplined program of prayer and personal devotion.

Group II: The committee and the church agreed that this group comes next; the order of priority within the group was different, but not significantly. The committee made certain these criteria are met, at least to some degree.

(1)6-8. A good steward of the financial resources God has given him.

(b)7-7. A man who has a vision for ministry to young people.

(i)8-6. A man able to maintain harmony within the church as it functions on a routine basis.

(n)9-9. A participant in visitation of new and prospective members.

(a)10-10. A man who visits regularly in the homes of members of the congregation. From the numbers, it would appear that the possession of a seminary degree fails with this second group of characteristics.

Group III: The committee and the church agreed that this group comes last. The committee should insure that a new pastor does not give highest priority to any of these.

(c)11-15. A leader qualified to head financial drives and building programs.

(j)12-13. A participant in denominational activities; able to represent denominational programs to the congregation.

(m)13-14. A participant in a disciplined program of continuing education.

(0)14-12. A community leader cooperative with social services and charitable programs.

(d)15-11. A participant in community activities.

INTERVIEW QUESTIONS

Developed by the Pastor Search Committee for
Pastoral Candidates Based on Profile

Group I:

(g). A man who preaches and teaches the Bible effectively: Biblical principles and practical guidelines for Christian living.

Questions:

1. How do you prepare a sermon?
2. How do you use the Bible in preparing to preach? What is the role of the Bible in preaching?
3. What is the most important use of the Bible in your life?
4. How and when should the pastor teach God's Word? Do you see yourself as primarily a teacher, or as a preacher, or as both? Please explain which you feel most capable of being and why.
5. Tell us about the best sermon you ever preached? the most difficult?
6. What do you see as the primary purpose of preaching?
7. How would you describe your preaching style?
8. How and when should the teaching of God's Word take place in the life of the church?

(f). A man who dialogues well with individuals about their spiritual development, religious life, and beliefs; counsels with people facing major decisions of life, e.g., marriage, and major crises and problems.

Questions:

1. What do you consider your personal responsibility with respect to evangelism? What methods, techniques, and scriptures do you use in evangelistic activities?
2. Have you ever sensed that you were God's instrument in leading someone to Christ? Please give a specific example? What scriptures, if any, did you use?
3. How would you encourage someone to spiritual growth?
4. If you had someone in the flock who was active in church, but involved in a lifestyle that did not abide by Christian principles, how would you handle the situation?
5. Why is pre-marital counseling important? How do you approach it?
6. Among your duties as a pastor, where does counseling rank as a priority?
7. How do you interpret the New Testament writings about divorce and/or remarriage?
8. Have you ever, in a counseling situation, come to the conclusion that divorce was the best solution? If yes, could you give examples of the types of situations which might lead you to advise a couple to get a divorce?
9. How would you guide someone in time of decision? Loneliness? Sorrow? Depression?
10. When is confidentiality important in counseling and when is it proper to share this kind of information? How do you share the fruits of your counseling ministry?
11. What are some of the characteristics that you consider important in a counselor?.
12. What would you ask a ten-year old who wanted to accept Jesus as Lord and Saviour?.

(e). A man who serves as an example of high moral and ethical character; cultivates a home and personal life with friends and interests outside local church activities.

Questions:

1. Does your current congregation know your political affiliation? How did they find out?
2. What is your stance on the issues of abortion? pornography? capital punishment? divorce? church discipline? Please explain your rationale.
3. What is the role of the church in government and public policy?
4. Is there a driving force in your life? If so, what is it?
5. Are there any things which you will not allow your children to do?
6. What is the most enriching part of your life?
7. What was the most meaningful part of your education? How are you continuing your formal education? Are you planning to pursue a doctorate? Why? Have you ever published anything? Have you received any honors not listed on your resume?
8. In all your ministry, what has disappointed you the most about people?
9. Have you learned to take counsel from others? How do you learn from others?
10. How do you normally react to someone who disagrees with you?
11. Have you ever refused to sign your name? If so, why?
12. Please tell us your position on alcohol, tobacco, and marijuana! Have you ever smoked either one?
13. What are your struggles in living as a godly man?
14. What are your car driving habits?
15. Name a few books you have read lately. What are your all-time favorites?
16. What movies have you seen recently? What are your all-time favorites?
17. Do you enjoy and attend/watch sports and cultural events? What are your preferences?
18. In what community activities are you currently participating?
19. What charitable programs do you currently support?
20. What para-church organizations do you support?
21. Do you practice what you preach?

(h). A man who meets the requirements set forth by the Apostle Paul in his letters: Titus 1:6-9 and 1 Timothy 3:1-7.

Questions: This one is unique because it is based on word study in the original Greek of the meaning of the words in the list of qualifications.

1. Blameless: with nothing laid to one's charge, not even the accusation. I Timothy 3:2, Titus 1:6

   a. Are there events in your past, either before you came to know the Lord or since that have been a hindrance to your ministry or could hinder a ministry with us?
   b. Do you have habits that some might find offensive?
   c. Is your immediate as well as your extended family supportive of your being a professional clergyman?
   d. Are there people in your past whom you have wronged and with whom you have not been reconciled? If so, have you made sufficient effort to be at peace with them?

2. Husband of one wife: I Timothy 3:2; Titus 1:6

    a. We have become increasingly aware of pastors who are struggling with keeping moral priority and have had to leave the ministry. Would you be willing to choose a few ordained men within our church body to whom you would hold yourself accountable?

3. Vigilant: sober, circumspect, discrete, abstain from wine. I Timothy 3:2; Titus 1:6

    a. Do you spend time alone with God each day?
    b. Could you share with us something that God has been teaching you lately?

4. Sober: self-control, discrete, temperate. 1 Timothy 3:2, Titus 1:8

    a. Have a list of qualities and ask the prospective pastor to put in order of greatest importance and rate himself in those qualities.

5. Good behaviour: fair, honest, valuable, virtuous.

    6. Given to hospitality: fond of guests. I Timothy 3:2; I Timothy 3:2; Titus 1:8

        a. Do you and your wife enjoy entertaining others in your home?

7. Apt to teach: instructive. I Timothy 3:2

    a. How do you get most of your ideas for sermons?
    b. What makes an individual qualified to teach God's word?

8. Not given to wine: in the vicinity of, casual. Titus 1:7

    a. Do you drink alcoholic beverages either privately or socially?

9. Not a striker: not a smiter, not pugnacious, not quarrelsome. I Timothy 3:3; Titus 1:7.

    a. How do you feel about what is presently taking place in the Southern Baptist Convention?
    b. What is your position regarding the inspiration of Scripture?

10. Not greedy of filthy lucre: without covetousness; without shameful gain. I Timothy 3:3.

11. Patient, not soon to anger: mild, gentle, appropriate. I Timothy 3:3; Titus 1:7.
    a. How strict are you about staying to a planned schedule?
    b. When someone interrupts your schedule, how do you react?

12. Not a brawler:

13. Not covetous:

14. Ruleth his own home:

(k). A man who maintains a disciplined program of prayer and personal devotion.

Questions:

1. Please share your testimony with us - orally and in writing.
2. Would you please tell us about your personal devotional life, materials you use for a quiet time, suggestions you might give others in establishing a meaningful daily time with the Lord, etc.?
3. What kind of prayer and devotional life do you have with your family? with your staff? with your deacons? What have you found to be an effective way of leading your family in family devotions: i.e., time of day, materials available for family devotions, other suggestions.
4. Regarding prayer:
   a. What priority should prayer have in the life of the church??
   b. How do you suggest a church develop an effective prayer ministry?
   c. What materials have you found to be beneficial in equipping an individual, group, or church to become victorious in prayer?.
   d. What are the benefits of prayer partnerships and prayer groups? Would you suggest ways of establishing such relationships?
   e. What successes and failures have you experienced in the area of prayer?.
   f. Would you tell us about the prayer groups in your present church? How would you describe the prayer life of your present church?
   g. Who has influenced you most in the area of prayer?.

Group II:

The committee and the church agree that this group comes next; the order of priority within the group was different, but not significantly. The committee should make certain these criteria are met, at least to some degree.

(l). A good steward of the financial resources God has given him.

Questions:

1. What do you teach about tithing? Do you tithe?
2. How do you and your family establish priorities for your finances?
3. Who actually pays the bills in your home?
4. Are you saving for retirement? for your children's education?
5. What provision have you made for your wife and family in the event of your untimely death?
6. What is your view of the use of credit cards?
7. Are you involved in any business ventures outside the Church?
8. If you felt called to the mission field, would indebtedness keep you from going?

(b). A man who has a vision for ministry to young people.

Questions:

1. How much hands-on involvement have you had in youth ministry?
2. What kind of staffing do you feel is important for truly effective youth and college ministry?
3. As the senior pastor of a church, how do you fit into youth ministry?
4. What types of Sunday School materials have you found to be effective? How would you react to the fact that the Sunday School teachers for Junior and Senior High students do not use Southern Baptist literature in their classrooms?
5. In what ways do you feel young people can contribute to the life of a church?
6. What type of para-church groups have effective ministries for youth?

(i). A man able to maintain harmony within the church as it functions on a routine basis.

Questions:

1. Have you ever been in a church that split? What caused the split? What was your involvement?
2. What do you do with a dispute or conflict between church members?
3. What kinds of plans would you have for the staff of this church?
4. What is the role of the church body in discipleship?
5. How do you disciple new believers?
6. What ministries in your present church are most effective and why? Which of those would be effective here? How would you go about implementing them here?
7. How best can the ministry of this church be shared among all its members?
8. Discuss the role of Sunday School and its structure in the life of the church.
9. Discuss the role of the deacons/board of deacons/diaconate in the church.
10. Discuss the role of women in the church.

(n). A participant in visitation of new and prospective members.
(a). A man who visits regularly in the homes of members of the congregation.

Questions: (combined)

1. How important is the visitation of prospective members? New members? Members?
2. Do you feel comfortable visiting in people's homes? Would you call first, or just drop in? Would you wait to be invited?
3. Are you comfortable with members visiting in your home?
4. Do you feel comfortable visiting in hospitals? Nursing homes?
5. What types of visits do you enjoy the most? the least?
6. In your opinion, who should be involved in the ministry of visitation? Pastor/Other staff members/Committees? How do you encourage people to become involved in visitation?
7. How would you implement a program of body ministry?

Group III:

The committee and the church agree that this group comes last. The committee should insure that a new pastor does not give highest priority to any of these.

(c). A leader qualified to head financial drives and building programs.

Questions

1. How do you feel about church indebtedness?
2. How should the church decide whether to build? Who in the church has the final word?
3. Have you ever been involved in or managed a building program?
4. How was it financed?
5. What did you learn from the experience?

(j). A participant in denominational activities; able to represent denominational programs to the congregation.

Questions:

1. How do you view the role of the local, state, and national associations/conventions of the Southern Baptist Convention?
2. What is the role of the local pastor in each association/convention?
3. What has been your role in the local association and state and national conventions?
4. Do you aspire to leadership in any of the conventions?
5. How do you inform your congregation of denominational matters?

(m). A participant in a disciplined program of continuing education.

Questions:

1. With a doctorate: are you continuing your education in any formal way?
2. Have you published? If so, what and where?
3. Have you received any honors not listed on your resume?
4. What are your plans for future education?

(0). A community leader who is (will be) cooperative with social services and charitable programs.

Questions:

1. How do you see the relationship between para-church and local church?
2. Which community activities are you participating in now? Why?
3. Which charitable program(s) are you at present supporting? How?
4. What para-church organization(s), if any, are you involved in?

(d). A participant in community activities.

Questions

1. In which community activities have you participated or would you enjoy participating?

MISSIONS QUESTIONS:

1. What kind of missions ministry is most appealing to you?
2. Aside from youth ministry in missions, how do you see this church's mission emphasis with respect to local association, state convention, mission churches, trips, the SBC?
3. What would you expect of the church missions committee?

VI. SOURCES FOR FURTHER SUGGESTIONS AND INFORMATION

American Baptist Churches. *Calling an American Baptist Minister and Church Reflections.* American Baptist Churches USA: Valley Forge, PA, 1991. (The American Baptist Church has compiled an exhaustive series of forms and questions designed to help the church analyze its needs, create an accurate church profile, interview pastoral candidates, make an offer, and orchestrate an installation ceremony.)

Chitwood, Michael. *Church Compliance System: How & Where to Start.* Corinthians Kingdom Publishing House: Chattanooga, Tenn., 1994.

Grubbs, Bruce. *The Pastor Selection Committee.* The Sunday School Board of the Southern Baptist Convention: Nashville, Tenn., 1977.

Hendricks, Garland. *The Ongoing of a Baptist Church: The Ethics and Etiquette of Calling A Pastor.* The B.C. Morris Academy for Christian Studies, Gardner-Webb College: Boiling Springs, NC, 1984.

Ketchum, Bunty. *So You're on the Search Committee.* The Alban Institute, Inc.: Washington DC, 1985. (The Alban Institute, a non-denominational organization, publishes a wide range of materials on issues of clergy roles and church life and church conflict.)

Lamb, Robert L. and Howell, Stan. *Workbook for Staff Minister Search Committees: A Guide for Seeking a Staff Minister.* Baptist State Convention of North Carolina: Cary, NC, 1991.

Pastor Church Relations. *Workbook for Search Committees.* Baptist State Convention: Cary, NC.

Oswald, Roy. *Finding Leaders For Tomorrow's Churches: The Growing Crisis in Clergy Recruitment.* The Alban Institute, Inc.: Washington DC, 1993.

Oswald, Roy. *New Beginnings: A Pastorate Start Up Workbook.* The Alban Institute, Inc.: Washington DC, 1989.

Phillips, Wm. Bud. *Pastoral Transitions: From Endings to New Beginnings.* The Alban Institute, Inc.: Washington DC, 1988.

C-2. CARE OF CHILDREN AND DEPENDENT CARE WORKERS

I. A HIGH RISK ARENA

If the hiring of clergy is the least regulated of any hiring context, we now consider the MOST regulated and vulnerable arena of all—the employment of persons to work with children and other dependent persons.

The risk of serious harm to such vulnerable persons is great, and society and the law is increasingly sensitive to this. Dependent care, which includes care for children, the elderly, and other dependent persons, is an area which calls for great care precisely because these persons are most susceptible and most vulnerable to abuse, and are the least able to reveal such abuse or defend against it. Their judgment may be impaired—certainly, their ability to control their environment is limited. They can't usually just walk away, call for help, or effectively defend themselves. In the case of abuse, the impression and emotional injury can be lasting. Some children reach adulthood without recovering from the trauma of such abuse. This emotional injury may also be heightened due to its infliction by a trusted church employee.

Incidents of child and elder abuse are tragically common, and the law is responding with increased regulation and by holding organizations liable under respondeat superior and negligent hiring theories. Churches as well as other organizations will be liable for harms caused to these dependent persons by both employees and volunteers. Indeed, a large share of the injuries inflicted by employees, and the resulting lawsuits, arise from within the dependent care arena.

While child abuse has received the most publicity, even the risks of injuries from simple ordinary negligence are often intensified. Children, the elderly, handicapped persons and other dependent persons are less able to recognize danger, or to cope on their own when confronted with a dangerous situation. Their judgment may be poor. Physically they may be more vulnerable to injuries from falls. They may not recognize dangers that others would easily avoid.

All dependent care facilities and workers must, therefore, exercise an increased sense of duty towards those placed in its care, and should take extra precautions in protecting their wards from harm.

II. CHURCHES AND DEPENDENT-CARE PROGRAMS

WARNING: YOU PROBABLY ARE INCLUDED.

Churches typically sponsor a number of dependent-care programs of various types. Churches may think they are not involved in such activity because they don't have a formal day-care program. However, such formal programs are not the only types of situations which involve care of dependent persons and where the heightened liability may be found.

In fact, most churches have at least some dependent-care programs. These often include a nursery, after-school child care, mothers' morning-out programs, tutoring programs, classes for the disabled or other "special" adults, scouting-type programs, youth and children's group events, and weekend youth retreats. Each of these, while not a "day-care" program, carries the same weighty moral obligations, many of the same inherent risks of harm, and similar liability to the church for ensuing injury that accompany the highly regulated day-care arena.

Such programs as day-care nursery care, mom's morning out, Backyard Bible Clubs, or scout-type activities are further complicated by two facts:

First, some programs are staffed by largely unsupervised volunteers (sometimes in part by persons not necessarily affiliated with the church congregation) and,

Second, some of the programs are patronized significantly by those outside the church community. Indeed, many of these programs lose their "church-family" feel and are instead more like businesses. This is especially true with pay-for-service day-care programs. This results in an increase in associated risks: workers are less well known, and patrons are unknown. More formal procedures for gathering appropriate information on such persons may be needed.

Volunteers present a particularly touchy subject in dependent care programs. Not only must the children and the elderly in these programs be protected from harm, but the church must be protected as well since it can be held liable if any injury does occur. Therefore, the church must be just as careful in selecting volunteers for these positions as it is for hiring full-time employees.

While the church, as a general rule, enjoys great freedom from government intervention in practicing its faith and running its organization, in these areas of heightened responsibility, however, the state has been more willing to enact regulations and to impose strict legal duties upon the church, and juries are less likely to look the other way. The church day-care carries the strictest statutory requirements, but all dependent care programs deserve careful analysis.

III. NECESSITY FOR EXTRA-SENSITIVE SCREENING OF EMPLOYEES

Because of the risks involved, employees hired by the church for any dependent-care position should be appropriately screened, utilizing the steps suggested in Section II. All steps should be completely and consistently implemented. The volunteers for such programs should be handled just as carefully. (See next section on volunteers.)

A. Assessing Range of Risks

Of course, the nature of the activity will control the scope of the screening of both employees and volunteers. The nature of the activity and the particular employee task will dictate the scope of screening. The following elements indicate a need for special care and increased scrutiny:

1. The extent to which the activity requires special skills—natural or by training—in order to accomplish the assigned task, and whether parents or others are relying on that expertise.

2. The extent to which the nature and scope of the activity suggests potential risks if the employee lacks the requisite character, judgment or experience.

3. The extent to which the activity itself may be inherently dangerous or risky

4. The degree of risk inherent in the activity. (Compare, for example, taking small children to a large amusement park, and having a Bible Drill with them at church during the evening service).

To the extent "high-risk" factors are present, the church should move toward requiring a full screening of volunteer workers. If no factors are present, relatively little screening of volunteers may be needed. This will become more clear as you proceed through this section.

Example: A church member volunteers to teach a weekly "crafts program" to the pre-school children in the church day-care. Should this person be screened? Minimally. There is little risk involved because the volunteer will not be alone with the children, the class will be taught at the church site, and the material or processes taught will not be dangerous to the children or volunteer.

Example: A church group conducts a regular class for special, handicapped adults. What screening should occur? This is a good example where the issue is not so much what each worker/volunteer must know, but rather the required resources in the group as a whole. If the group is dealing with disabled persons, there must be someone with enough knowledge of the disabilities and likely emergencies that they may deal with them properly. Also, the facilities and resources must be used appropriately for this group.

Example: A staff member of the church is assigned responsibility for developing a program for 2-4 year olds on a once a week mom's morning-out program. What screening should be done? Here some substantial screening should be involved, especially if this person will design and implement the program with the help of volunteers. Are they experienced with this age group? Are they trained in first aid? Are they by temperament a risk in handling children of this age group being left by their mothers? Can they develop appropriate activities? And, a critical question, is this person able, along with volunteers, to properly supervise the activity? All of these questions must be satisfactorily addressed.

B. Areas Warranting Special Concern for Churches

Applying some of the tests above, the common church programs which would warrant some special concerns for the qualifications and character of employees and volunteers would include the following:

1. Formal day-care programs
2. Other child-care supervision for extended periods: e.g., Mom's Morning Out
3. Church nurseries
4. Overnight activities with small children—e.g., camping
5. Youth excursions, ovenights and camping activities
6. Disabled and "special adult" programs involving transportation and supervision
7. Elder-care activities
8. High risk activities with minors—e.g., canoeing
9. Foreign travel with minors

IV. PERSONNEL AND OTHER OPERATING POLICIES

While appropriate hiring and screening greatly decrease the risks inherent in dependent care programs, the most critical issues often arise AFTER employment, and beyond the scope of this Hiring Guide. These post-hiring issues relate largely to personnel and operating policies, which seek to assure a safe and healthy environment.

Consider, for example, a church nursery. Obviously, WHO works in the nursery (whether an employee or a volunteer) is very important. Screening for competence, maturity, and experience with handling infants and toddlers would be legitimate, as would assurances that workers are not a personal danger to the children because of violence or abuse. Indeed, a church might well have a brief Form for Nursery Volunteers—a sort of supplemental application form.

But such screening is only the first step, and itself may be imperfect. A further way to assure an appropriate nursery staff situation is by additional policies covering such matters as the following:

- Number of persons who must always be present in nursery
  Many churches have requirements that no worker may be with small children alone, both to protect against actual or alleged abuse, and to assure that emergencies can be handled properly.
- Adequate number of persons depending on the size of the group
- Staff knowledge and training to handle emergencies
- Procedures to avoid releasing a child to someone who does not have the right to the child. Some large churches have formal procedures to assure that the person who brought the child is the one who picks up the child.
- Procedures for handling children with diseases or injuries
- Policies preventing persons with infectious diseases from working in the nursery
- Policies about handling body fluids, waste
- Policies for handling complaints about the care of any child
- Policies indicating who has authority for certain kinds of actions, e.g., discipline, sending children home, and getting medical services.

Such policies not only provide a safer environment, but also help deal with some of the inherent limits in dealing with non-professional volunteers.

V. DAY-CARE PROGRAMS

A. Unique Aspects

Formal day-care programs are the most highly regulated programs run by the church. (The State even has a definition of "day-care programs" which may encompass some church children's activities that the church would not have thought were "day-care.") This is appropriate because of the special aspects which distinguish them from the typical children's church programs. Consider the distinctions:

1. Consider, first, the large role they play in the lives of these youngsters. These programs often involve the most time with the children, often supervising children for 40-50 hours per week, rather than for the shorter, less frequent duration of other

programs. The workers in this environment are often more like primary care providers than simply baby-sitters or program leaders.

2. Day-care programs are also frequently offered to the general public. This justifies the state's regulation of such services, and maintaining minimum standards for such facilities. Because of the amount of attention given to these programs by the state, day-care programs will be addressed separately here. Keep in mind that what the state considers good practices for a day-care might also be good practices for other church programs. And, in fact, a church may be considered negligent or unreasonable in not incorporating such practices into its other programs, though other programs are not specifically regulated by the state.

3. Further, unlike local church youth and children's programs, the parents of the children themselves often have little direct involvement. A church boys' program, for example, probably involves at least some of the boys' parents who, in at least most churches, know the other parents on both a church and social basis. In day-care programs, however, the parents' involvement and knowledge of the workers is rather limited.

B. State Day-Care Staffing Regulations

Many churches have become involved in licensed day-care programs. These are typically staffed by paid employees. Because of the growing need for such programs, and concerns with quality, there are various professional associations and other agencies which provide extensive resources on developing quality programs, achieving state standards, and on staffing issues. It is not our purpose here to replicate all the helpful counsel such state and private agencies and organizations provide, but to highlight some of the major aspects which relate to general policy and legal issues.

Child-care facilities are regulated on a state, not national, level, though states may comply with suggested federal guidelines in order to qualify for grants. Some counties and cities mandate additional requirements. Each church must check the appropriate laws covering its facility, though most are similar. To demonstrate some of the most necessary and most common regulations, North Carolina law will be used.

There are numerous regulations regarding child-care facilities which are applicable to the physical environment, reporting requirements, and other administrative areas, but these are beyond our scope here; we are more concerned with the hiring/staffing requirements. Most states, including North Carolina, exempt day-care facilities sponsored by religious organizations from some of the staffing requirements applied to others. Most such exemptions pertain to on-going training, experience, and educational requirements. Other minimal standards are applicable to religious as well as non-religious facilities. Many churches which could be licensed under the less demanding church standards choose nevertheless to seek licensing under the more stringent requirements.

The minimum standards attributable to religious day-care facilities can be broken down into two categories:

    (1) those that pertain to all workers, meaning both hired employees and volunteers, and
    (2) those that pertain only to "employees".

N.C. Requirements:

1. Age

All workers must be 16 years of age to be counted in the "staff per child" head count. If the person will not be counted as "staff" for purposes of meeting the state-required staff per child, there is no age requirement.

Example: State X requires that each child care facility maintain a staff person for every five children. The church child care has fifteen children. There are two adults of twenty-one years or older as well as three fifteen year-old teenagers on duty. Has the church met the requirements?

No. Only those over the age of sixteen can be counted as "staff". Therefore, only two "staff" are counted on site. Three are required here.

2. Supervisor Requirements

The facility supervisor or director must be literate and at least 21 years of age.

3. Operator

An "operator" of the facility, whether an employee or a volunteer, must be free from criminal conviction for a list of specified crimes (child neglect, child abuse, moral turpitude, excessive alcohol use, or drug use).

4. Employeee Requirements

All "employees" are required to be free from the above specified crimes regardless of their position within the facility. Both employees and facility operators must be free of mental or emotional impairment which might be injurious to children.

C. Special Screening Concerns for Day-Care Employees

In addition to following the standard hiring procedures outlined in Steps 1-10 within this text, the following additions are of critical importance in hiring child-care workers. These suggestions are recommended for both volunteers and employees; but in the event this is not possible, the church should certainly implement the whole process for all workers in designated "high-risk" positions.

1. Criminal record checks:

Criminal record checks on child-care workers is required by law in most states, and even if not required by a particular state, it would be deemed "unreasonable" and "negligent" even in those states for a church to hire a child care worker without running such a check.

North Carolina, as well as most states, requires that child care workers be free from convictions for child neglect, child abuse, moral turpitude, any drug use, or use of excessive alcohol. [NCGS sec. 110-91] In order for a church or employer to determine that there is indeed no record of such conviction, a criminal record check should be run. (See previous section on how to run a criminal record check.)

The church or day-care provider will also be responsible for updating its information periodically. While no set time frame is established for this process, the church/employer would clearly be negligent for continuing to employ a worker who has acquired (even unbeknownst to the church) a record for any such abuse, so the church must be careful to update and to document such information regularly. Such procedures should be established ahead of time and implemented and followed without exception. It would be good policy to update the checks at least annually.

Furthermore, in the event that the church ends up defending itself in a negligent hiring legal suit, the church must be able to produce documentation to show that it took reasonable care in hiring and continuing to employ the employee. The criminal record check is an integral part of this documentation, so great care should be maintained in properly acquiring and storing such information.

> *Example: A child is seriously injured by a church worker who is attempting to discipline the child. There is no state requirement that child care workers' criminal records be checked, so the church did not check one here. The worker has a long history: He was abused as a child and has several convictions for child abuse. Could the church be liable?*
>
> *Very likely. The church did not exercise "due care" in hiring this employee. "Due care" does NOT mean merely meeting the legal requirements for hiring; it also means being reasonable in uncovering pertinent information before hiring an employee and entrusting him with particular duties.*

2. Drug and alcohol testing:

North Carolina, like most states, requires that child-care workers be free from convictions for drug use or excessive alcohol use. Although the statute addresses "convictions" for drug and alcohol abuse, the state has clearly set forth its concern over the use of such substances in the child care setting.

While only a criminal record check will determine the "conviction" of a worker for such abuses, running a drug test as part of the standard hiring procedure is clearly necessary to determine whether or not there is any active drug use (although the applicant may be free of "convictions" for such use). The state has clearly indicated its dissatisfaction with the employment of substance abusers in this context, so it is not a stretch to assume that the court would find an employer who did not monitor for such abuse to be "unreasonable" and "negligent".

A regular testing of employees for drug use or on-site alcohol use is recommended. This is, of course, subject to the employer's discretion, but if there is any indication of irregularity at all, the church/employer would be highly suspect in not substantiating and eliminating this concern.

Random or regular drug and alcohol testing should be spelled out in the church rules and policies. This will ensure that all employees are aware of such policies and are not subject to arbitrary or harassing tests. Discrimination claims could easily arise without such documented standardization.

If tests are run, again, document everything. As with any other documentation, a negative result is just as conclusive as a positive result in substantiating that appropriate steps and safeguards were implemented by the church.

3. Medical tests and exams:

Most states also maintains minimum health requirements for all child-care workers (although some workers in religious sponsored facilities may be exempt from many such requirements). All employees must submit to a pre-employment medical exam as well as annual TB tests. All employees must also submit a medical statement or health questionnaire annually.

Document everything. The employer cannot be held liable for not knowing information it diligently sought but was unable to obtain.

An additional area of concern under the medical testing area is that of the *gathering* of medical information. Just as the employer may not request a medical *exam* before the offer, the employer may not ask medical *questions* of the applicant before the offer. This includes such questions as whether or not the applicant is suffering from any major illness or is HIV positive.

Of course, the employer may ask whether or not the applicant is able to perform the essential functions of the job. If the applicant's illness prevents him/her from performing such functions, and a reasonable accommodation cannot reasonably be made which would enable him/her to do so, that applicant may be eliminated from consideration based on a bona fide occupational qualification.

4. AIDS issues in hiring:

One of the complex legal and policy questions today is the employer's obligation toward those those with AIDS. For the religious employer, this may be a particularly sticky subject. The issue involves not only legal questions, but theological and practical ones.

On the one hand, the church sees its role as a compassionate source of support for all victims of devastating illnesses. The Christian community has a long and noble tradition of reaching out to the outcase. AIDS victims, at least socially, seem closely akin to the lepers of Jesus' day. Many churches have developed specific ministries to AIDS victims. Many with AIDS may have becomes its victims even without participating in the homsexual or drug use conduct which most churches would condemn.

On the other hand, churches may see employment as a quite different issue from compassion. The church may want to draw distinctions based on how a person contracted AIDS. And regardless of how churches may view the issues theologically or theoretically, certainly parents of children or youth will take strong exception if persons who are HIV-positive were working closely with their children, or in other activities such as sports where injuries and contact with body fluids was a significant possibility.

AIDS—The Law

First, HIV is treated as any other disability under the Americans with Disabilities Act. An organization which falls within the jurisdiction of the ADA (15 or more employees) cannot discriminate against a handicapped person. Thus, the organization may not discriminate against AIDS victims. The law makes no distinction between types of disabilities. (Note: Many churches would draw a disticntion between those "handicaps" that are not the result of personal choices, and those that are self-induced — drug addiction, HIV. The latter are conduct-based, and churches often believe the underlying conduct was "sin," and that the law, in effect, ignores this distinction.)

[The Civil Rights Act, which does cover many churches, is another possible refuge for the AIDS victim. However, at this time, neither sexual orientation nor homosexuality is a protected class, so even if a church is covered by the Civil Rights Act, it is not prohibited from discriminating based on these factors. Unless a corresponding state law does consider them a protected class, the church will still be free to implement its own hiring policy.]

Does all this mean the church has no recourse, and must, in fact, hire homosexual AIDS carriers even in its day care program?

Not necessarily.

First, if, the church is not within the jurisdiction of the ADA, it has no legal obligation to comply with the ADA rules. It will then be up to the individual church to establish rules and procedures for handling cases which might arise. Considering the vast number of AIDS cases which are projected to rise by the year 2000, the development of such a policy may require careful analysis.

Second, even if the church is covered by the ADA, if the church has established that it has sincerely-held religious beliefs based on a religious doctrine central to its practice which prohibits it from hiring persons who are involved in homosexual activity, it may have a strong case for refusing to hire them—not on the basis of AIDS, but because of their conduct. Or, if the church, based on these same beliefs, develops standard codes of conduct or ethics which all employees are required to abide by, and one of these rules prohibits homosexual conduct, it may also have a strong case. This is a very murky area of law at this time, since it pits the First Amendment Establishment Clause and the Free Exercise of Religion against the federally mandated employment discrimination acts. We will not know what the outcome of such a dispute will be until a case is settled by the Supreme Court, which may be years from now.

Third, if the church did find itself prohibited by either federal or state law from discriminating against persons with AIDS, and it had no other religious doctrine which prohibited it from hiring such persons, another consideration may still arise. In the hiring of day-care workers, there may be an exception. Most states, including North Carolina, require annual physical exams, and do not permit those with contagious diseases to work with children. Although in most cases AIDS cannot be casually transmitted, working with children may create a greater risk. Children are precocious, unpredictable, and more likely to bite or scratch each other or the child care provider, or in other foreseeable ways facilitate the transference of blood or body fluids. Based on these risks, an organization would probably have a firm case in refusing to hire day-care workers, or in similar situations, dependent care workers, who are HIV positive. Certainly most churches would be convinced that in the day care context they had a reasonable, even compelling, health reason to discriminate against those who were HIV+, and would thus refuse to hire such persons on the same basis they would refuse to hire an applicant with any other communicable disease. North Carolina, for example, has a statute which prohibits the employer from testing for AIDS in order to determine suitability for *continued* employment. However, the statute specifically allows the employer to require an AIDS test as part of a pre-employment medical examination, and allows the employer to deny employment ". . . to a job applicant based solely on a confirmed positive test. . . ." Further, the employer is permitted to reassign or terminate an employee if his/her infection would pose a significant risk to others or is unable to perform the duties of the job. NCGS § 130A-148.

The "Bottom Line"

Most churches would, quite properly we believe, rather risk an employment law suit than put children at risk, and will, therefore, decline to hire persons with any serious communicable diseases including AIDS.

5. Transportation:

North Carolina requires a valid driver's license for the type of vehicle used to transport the children. The statute does not state requirements for the driver's record, but it can be assumed that a good driving record would be of great importance in employing a driver.

The insurance carrier covering the facility's vehicle will require notification of all drivers who may be driving it. The insurer will be expected to cover all such drivers. If the insurer uncovers a poor driving record for someone who has been submitted as a potential driver of the vehicle, the insurer will likely refuse to extend coverage to this driver. An applicant's poor driving record will then be revealed, and the employer should take care to restrict this person to non-driving positions, even if he would be willing to drive his own vehicle. Once the church is put on notice of the poor driving record, it would be negligent in authorizing any driving by such an individual on its behalf.

A "gray area" arises when the employee is asked to drive for the church on an irregular or informal basis, and driving is not part of the employee's regular duties. The employee will most likely be driving his own vehicle and will usually be volunteering or requested to transport children or church members to a church-sponsored event. Because the employee was not offered a "driver" position at the on-set, this person's driving record would not have been cleared by the insurer and would basically be unknown. This is a dangerous situation. If any child-care worker may potentially be driving or shuttling children for any reason, a driver's record check should be run upon hiring and regularly thereafter.

A court of law would consider it "unreasonable" and "negligent" to allow an employee with a poor driving record to drive others. The church must be aware of this and implement an easy record checking policy that it follows without fail and updates regularly. (For more information on how to run such a check, see previous Section.)

> *Example: An applicant applies for the church bus driver position. Although an otherwise excellent candidate, the church's insurer will not cover him due to the many accidents on his record. The applicant is instead hired to help in another area of the church. The church later asks for volunteers to drive groups of seniors to a church-sponsored function. This employee volunteers and has an accident enroute. Could the church be liable?*

> *Yes. The church had notice of this employee's poor driving record. At a minimum, the church had a duty to inform those riding with him of the inherent risk. The church should have taken the safer route and refused to allow him to drive in any church-related capacity.*

6. Discipline:

The state of North Carolina prohibits the use of corporal punishment except in religious-sponsored facilities operating under the provisions of G.S. 110-106. Further, discipline may not be related to food, rest, or toileting; children may not be locked up; discipline may not be delegated to another child; and the facility's discipline policy must be provided to parents in writing.

While these discipline guidelines may have no negligent hiring ramifications, it may be important to note that an employee's conduct must be within the guidelines of the statute or the exception. The employee's willingness to function within the guidelines themselves should be thoroughly reviewed in the interview.

7. *Walking through the process of hiring child care workers:*

Again, utilizing the complete hiring process as well as the additional safeguards for all child care workers, whether permanent or volunteer, is recommended. If this is not possible, volunteers should be screened as outlined under "Volunteers" (See next chapter.) and volunteers for high-risk positions as well as all church employees should be subject to the complete process, including the aforementioned additions.

To make sure all available steps are completed and appropriate safeguards are taken, utilize the "Checklist" described in Step 10.

In addition, the supplemental questions included on the Child Care Interview Supplement in the Appendix should be utilized. Most of these questions are aimed at uncovering information that may only be relevant in such a setting.

D. Use of Volunteers in Day-Care

1. Classification of Volunteers

Classifying the worker as an "employee" or "volunteer" and then only meeting the minimum legal screening requirements for each will, of course, not ensure the safety of the children or the church's freedom from liability for resulting injury. As discussed in the "volunteer" section, a volunteer can at times be deemed an "employee" by the court even if the church considers him a volunteer. In such a case, the employer (church) would be still liable for the injury inflicted by the volunteer.

Because it is difficult to accurately predict the circumstances under which the court will classify the worker as an "employee" rather than a "volunteer", it is important to review the minimum requirements for permanent day-care workers ("employees") and then expand them to include volunteers where high-risk factors are present. This will reduce the risk of injury to the children as well as the resulting liability to the church.

2. Screening Volunteers

As repeated many times within this text, treating volunteers as permanent employees during the hiring process and beyond is highly recommended. A thorough screening process offers the church the greatest opportunity to competently screen and select candidates for positions and to thus foresee and avoid injurious conduct which often results in legal liability. In many cases, however, the church is unwilling to expend the effort to include volunteers in such a process, or the church simply does not have the resources to screen all volunteers as thoroughly as it does its employees.

The church day-care facility is one area in which a large number of volunteers contribute their time on a regular or sporadic basis. There is often great turnover in the bulk of the volunteer work force, and workers come and go leaving little, if any, paper trail.

The great potential for personal injury and resulting liability in the day-care setting makes it important to closely evaluate the church's hiring practices. In certain high-risk situations it is imperative that volunteers be as thoroughly screened as the day-care employees are, even if this is not the standard practice for all church volunteer positions.

3. Identifying the High Risk Contexts

High-risk situations are those which indicate a great potential for injury to others. Such situations dictate that "due care" be used in hiring all workers (employees and volunteers), and that such efforts be documented. Thorough and consistent hiring procedures are key in establishing that the church used due care.

Answering "yes" to the following questions should raise "red flags". The church should closely evaluate its hiring practices for all workers; volunteer hiring practices should be adjusted accordingly.

High-risk factors:

- Are day-care workers likely to be left alone with children even if the church has a policy of requiring more than one worker in the facility at a time?

- Even if there are other workers present, is there opportunity for a worker to be alone with a child for any period of time?

- Does the facility supervisor have time to oversee the activities of the volunteers while they are working, or is he really too busy caring for children as well?

- Is there time for necessary training or instruction for inexperienced volunteer help, or is the volunteer expected to come prepared and able to handle the position, even if the volunteer has not been screened based on experience?

- If training is needed and the supervisor does not have the time or resources available to train, the church would probably be negligent in allowing untrained/inexperienced workers into such a situation.

- Is the facility very hectic, with each worker expected to handle a certain number of children with little attention from others?

- Could certain play equipment (playgrounds, etc.) be dangerous for children not closely supervised by a trained or experienced child-care provider?

- If youth are involved, will there be off-site activities which the volunteer will be expected to attend? (How well supervised are these?)

If the answer to any of the above is "yes", there is a clear indication that any worker must be well-trained, experienced, or (in the case of the first three questions) documented to be without a history of child abuse or related crimes. Allowing an unscreened or inappropriate worker into such an environment could easily result in injury to a child. Legal liability for such actions would be attributable to the church, who did not use due care in averting an obvious danger.

E. Other Hiring Issues in Day-Care Context for Churches

1. May a church selectively hire day-care workers on the basis of their religious faith?

Yes, as we noted in Step #1 in the preceding section, churches may preferentially select employees on the basis of their religious beliefs and commitments. It is true that many church day-care programs unfortunately seem totally secular in program and have little connection to the faith of the church other than using its facilities. In such cases, the right to invoke the religious exception may at some point be diminished. Some cases in the last few years have suggested that merely invoking religion or mere ownership of an activity by a church does not always guarantee the exemption. Churches would do well, in our opinion, as a matter of theology as well as law, to assure that church day-care programs reflect, in program and staff, the spiritual and religious commitments of the community and not function simply as a business. This will also protect the church against claims which have occurred in at least one major North Carolina city challenged the tax exemption of church property used for a day-care.

2. *May a church Day-Care require all of its employees and/or volunteers to be church members?*

Yes.

3. *May a church day-care require its employees and or volunteers to adhere to standards of personal conduct which are related to the church doctrine and faith?*

Yes.

Child Care Interview Supplement Questions

Statistics:

- Are you sixteen years of age or older?
- Are you twenty-one years of age or older if applying for a supervisory or director position?
- If applying for a supervisory or director position, are you literate?

Experience:

- What experience have you had working with children?
- What ages were the children you worked with?
- What did you like best about it?
- What did you like least about it?
- How many children did you work with at once?
- Were you comfortable with this workload?
- What number would you be most comfortable supervising?
- What age group are you least comfortable working with? Why?
- What would make you more comfortable working with this age group?
- Do you feel more comfortable working in a calm environment?
- How do you feel about working in a hectic environment?
- Do you tend to lose patience when work is chaotic?

Training:

- What formal training, if any, have you had which would relate to this position? When?
- What informal training, if any, have you had which would relate to this position? When?
- What additional training could we offer you that would better prepare you for this position?
- What additional training could we offer you that would increase your job-related skills?
- Would you be willing to take advantage of such training?

Personal Background:

- Please describe the relationship among your family members as you were growing up.
- What disciplinary measures were utilized?
- What type of discipline do you feel is most effective?
- Have you ever been physically or sexually abused?
- Have you ever been arrested, charged, convicted or had any unanswered allegations of accusations of any type made against you in regard to any misconduct toward children, or any physical or sexual abuse of children?

Such questions should allow the interviewer to uncover personality traits which might be better suited for other work within the church. These questions might also reveal weaknesses in experience or training which make this person a risky applicant for certain high-risk positions.

Some of the questions have also been included in some form in the standard Interview Form. But, to make sure the questions were fully answered as they pertain to the child care environment, they have been included here as well. If the answer has been given, simply note "see above" in the space provided for the answer. It will be better to ask the question twice than to overlook getting an answer.

The question, *"Have you ever been arrested, charged, convicted, or had any unanswered allegations or accusations of any type made against you in regard to **any** misconduct towards children, any physical or sexual abuse of children, or any misconduct of any type towards others? Please explain."* is extremely important in the day-care environment. Although we generally give applicants the benefit of believing them innocent until proven guilty, and thus only ask about "convictions" on the general application, the day-care applicant must be scrutinized more closely.

Oftentimes, the victims of sexual or physical abuse are reluctant or embarrassed to face their assailant, or to pursue remedies in court. The victim seeks an acknowledgment of the harm inflicted and a sincere apology—he wants to see regret by the perpetrator, not an ugly court battle. Because many of these cases are then settled outside the court system, convictions of such crimes may constitute a very small percentage of the crimes actually committed. Asking only about the applicant's convictions, then, may not be digging far enough. The jury may expect more from a "reasonable" employer.

Once all information is gathered, evaluate the applicant's qualifications thoroughly before giving him reign in the precious child-care environment. Your care and thoroughness will be well rewarded.

I. KEY FACT # 1: SCOPE OF VOLUNTEERS IN CHURCH PROGRAMS

II. KEY FACT # 2: RISKY BUSINESS!

III. THE LEGAL STATUS OF VOLUNTEERS

IV. PRACTICAL PROBLEMS FOR CHURCHES

V. A CHURCH RESPONSE TO VOLUNTEER SCREENING PROBLEMS

A long-time church member volunteers to drive van loads of children to and from church camp daily for a two-week period. During one of the trips, he is involved in an accident, and it is later determined that he was exceeding the speed limit and driving recklessly. The parents of an injured child sue the church for negligent hiring. Could this case succeed?

Yes. In this case, if the volunteer had a very poor driving record (which the church could have easily uncovered, as described within), the court may hold the church liable for negligent hiring. The classification of the worker as "volunteer" is irrelevant in a court of law. The church will be held to the same standards of care in "hiring" volunteers as it is for hiring permanent workers.

Many legal problems associated with employment can be avoided by implementing the sound hiring policies suggested in this Guide. Often the law or the hiring process itself discusses "employees." But who is an "employee"? And what about volunteers? Are they included? If so, must the employer extend the same care in hiring them? Will the employer be subject to the same legal liabilities as a result of their actions as with a permanent "employee"?

Most churches and non-profit organizations rely heavily on volunteers to supplement their full-time work force and to enable the organization to implement additional ministerial programs through the use of this added manpower; budgeting constraints often make this the ONLY source of personnel available for such noteworthy programs. This heavy use of volunteers is not likely to change in the near future.

I. KEY FACT # 1: SCOPE OF VOLUNTEERS IN CHURCH PROGRAMS

It is apparent that in fact MOST of the programs and activities of the church are really carried out by volunteers, not formal employees. Consider just some of the situations where volunteers do in churches what "employees" would be doing in other organizations:

Teaching adults and children
Supervising recreational activities
Cooking
Providing transportation
Building
Cleaning up the property
Maintenance of the facility
Yard work
Taking youth or senior adults on outings
Acting as camp supervisor or counselor
Musician
Mission work involving construction
Relief work in emergencies or natural disasters
Providing emergency food service

Managing a charitable thrift store
Working with youth in programs like Scouts,
       GA's, Boys Brigade, etc.
Helping the handicapped
Handling church funds
Picking up supplies for the church
Delivering pizza to the youth group
Supervising a lock-in
Assisting employees in programs like day-care
Taking care of the nursery during church
Vacation Bible School worker
Office-work volunteer
Custodian
Committee Work

II. KEY FACT # 2: RISKY BUSINESS!

Many of these activities create substantial risks of harm to others if they are not done properly.

Some of the activities on the list above pose especially high risks, e.g., operating a motor vehicle, working with children and other dependents, handling food, overnight supervision of children or youth, and working with power tools. In fact, with the exception of day-care employees, the most common risks from church activities arise from the activities of volunteers, not employees. The volunteer van driver is a far greater risk than the church secretary.

III. THE LEGAL STATUS OF VOLUNTEERS

These two facts about the scope of volunteer activities are especially significant given the legal context.

A. Legal Fact 1 - Liability for Volunteer Negligence

Churches and religious organizations often do not consider that the church is, in most instances, just as liable for the acts of volunteers as for employees. When a volunteer drives the church van, he is driving it FOR THE CHURCH. It makes no difference that he is not paid; it is still on behalf of the church. The law would view the driver as an agent (the old word was "Servant") of the church which is the principal (or "Master"). We have already noted in Section I that the Master is liable for the acts of the Servant when those acts are committed within the scope and course of the work of the Master. This is the *respondeat superior* type of liability.

The church, therefore, ought to be quite concerned about potential negligence and resulting harms from volunteers, just as it would from employees.

B. Legal Fact 2 - Liability for Church Negligence in Selecting Volunteers

The liability is also essentially the same under the negligent hiring types of liabilities. Further, an employer may be liable for the acts of its employees and volunteers if the employer fails to exercise due care in screening, hiring, or supervising such employees and volunteers.

If a church selects and appoints someone to work with the children whom the church knew or should have known was not competent or in some other way posed an unreasonable risk of harm, the church may well be liable for any harm caused the children. Consider these days the potential risks with volunteers in day-care programs, nurseries, and supervision of children and youth.

Churches must realize that the law does not differentiate between permanent and volunteer workers when considering a negligent hiring suit. The same standard of care is required from the employer for both. This means that when a church "hires", or utilizes, a volunteer worker, it must take reasonable care in determining that the volunteer is indeed qualified and poses no ascertainable threat to others.

IV. PRACTICAL PROBLEMS FOR CHURCHES

All this is made even more complex by the practical realities of church life.

A. Limited Resources

First, churches have limited resources and limited staff members available to extend the hiring process used for permanent hires to volunteer workers. Many churches feel that the burden of implementing such a process would simply require the reduction in the use of volunteers.

When a permanent position is filled, the employer identifies the inherent risk in the position (for example, that the person will be unsupervised while having access to youth) and does a correspondingly thorough background check. The greater the potential risk to others, the more thorough the check. This extensive care protects others from harm and gives the church comfort in knowing that it has selected the most qualified candidate, or at least that the person the church has employed will pose no danger to the church or others.

When a volunteer worker is added, on the other hand, often little is known of his background or experience. Most churches operate on trust and blind faith, and are grateful for the additional helping hands. In most cases, this is adequate. In the few startling exceptions, disaster results.

B. A Transitory and Episodic Volunteer Force

Second, the church may feel that the relatively episodic nature of volunteer work and the constant turnover of volunteer workers make it impossible to keep up with the process and paperwork of any "hiring" type review. When a volunteer is needed to go this weekend to help in tornado-relief work or to go right now to get some donuts for the overnight of the youth group, there is no the time for any "hiring" process, and even if there were it wouldn't be worth spending scores of hours to "qualify" the volunteer for a task that may take much less time than the review would.

C. Volunteer Resistance to A "Qualifying" Process

Third, recruiting workers is hard enough without eliminating some who won't take the time to go through the process. Few volunteers are going to take the time to fill out applications, provide release forms, or anything of that sort. It's tough enough to get them to raise their hand, or put their name on the sign-up sheet in the foyer.

D. It Would be Perceived as an Insult

Fourth, many volunteers might well take personal exception to any suggestion that they need to be investigated or checked out by some person or committee. This is exacerbated by the fact that churches thrive as communities of considerable mutual trust and fellowship. Any process which suggests that people couldn't be trusted would be destructive of central values of the church.

E. Our Mobile Communities

Fifth, the fact is that today churches are often made up of people who have not grown up together with years of personal and community relations. Churches are often made up of strangers whom we want to become involved. The irony is that this fact in some ways suggests we may need to be more careful about volunteers because we do NOT know much about many of the members. But the same facts make it more difficult. Any serious hiring-type process that really was intended to check out volunteers would today involve many more people than it would have in the more stable communities of a few generations ago.

V. A CHURCH RESPONSE TO VOLUNTEER SCREENING PROBLEMS

So what can a church do to effectively avoid the serious risks in some activities without destroying the sense of community or creating a management monster? Are there any options the church has in shortening the hiring process for volunteers while still screening effectively? In most cases, any shortcuts in the system result in a decrease in the effectiveness of the screening, but for practical purposes, a church should probably explore the following process:

A. Assess the Responsibilities and Risks Associated with Volunteer Activities

As our prior list of volunteer activities in a church quickly suggests, not all volunteers have the same levels of responsibility or pose the same kinds or degrees of risk. Volunteers to help weed the yard, paint the sanctuary, or teach an adult Sunday School class pose few risks of serious injury to themselves or others. Other types of volunteer activities pose much more serious risks because of one or both of two factors:

1. The vulnerability of those whose activities they will assist in, and/or
2. The inherent danger or risks of the activity itself — using a chain saw, driving a car

One might even create a scale of such activities according to the presence of one or both of these factors and note the kinds of activities of volunteers. It might look in a typical church something like this:

Low Risk	Moderate Risk	High Risk
Adult S.S. Teacher	Church Meals Cook	Day-care Volunteer
Church Clean-Up Day	Relief-Work Volunteer	Children's Camp Counselor
Office Work	Church Nursery Attendant	Church Van Driver

B. Consider the NATURE of the Risks the Volunteer Activity Creates

Next, for those positions involving moderate or substantial risk, consider whether the risks arise because of the potential dangers in the job itself, such as driving, or whether the risks are because of vulnerability of the recipients.

The importance of this distinction is that in the former case, the issues of careful selection (hiring, if you will) are usually limited to questions of the competence (training, aptitude, skills) in the specific task involved. In the second instance, it is not so much the presence or lack of a specific skills as it is questions of general character, maturity, judgment, etc.

Examples

For example, if the volunteer is to operate a motor vehicle for the church (taking youth to camp, picking up special adults), the chief risk posed relates directly to one issue: is the person an appropriate person to choose as a driver? We don't need to know much about character, educational background, or whether he was a victim of child abuse. We DO need to know whether the person is a driving risk, and to know that we need to know one basic thing: What is his driving record? Is there anything in that record, or reports from others who have witnessed his driving, that would warn the church so that to accept him as a driver would be "negligent."

Similarly, if the volunteer is to go on a tornado-relief work project, it would depend on what type of volunteer work he would do. Suppose he were to clean up brush. Then probably no special "selectivity" would be mandated. If, however, he were going to operate a chain saw, it might be important to know if he had any experience with a chain saw — its operation and dangers.

Consider alternatively the situation with a nursery worker or child-care volunteer, or overnight children's camp supervisor. In this situation, we are not just interested in skills. The church, and the parents of all those involved, would probably like to be assured the person is a responsible adult, exercises good judgment, knows how to appropriately discipline, has minimal health care skills, and in today's world, we'd like to be sure the person is not an undue risk of physical, sexual or other abuse to those in his care. This is a rather broad set of concerns, unlike the chain saw skills question.

Summary of Questions

Thus, we have now suggested two important inquiries:

First, does the volunteer create some significant level of risk that warrants at least SOME screening.

Second, given the nature of the risks, what kind of screening is reasonably expected.

Example: The church requests volunteers to meet at the local park and help clean it up. Is screening needed? Probably not. There is very little danger and few skills are needed for such work.

Example: The church is building a home for a homeless family. The church requests volunteers to help roof the house. Is screening needed? Some. Specific skills are needed, and the height involved makes the position more risky to the individuals. The church should only utilize those with experience. A check into the volunteer's personal background, however, is not necessary.

Example: The church is having a cookout. It requests volunteers to help cook. Is screening needed? Some. Again, the cooking could be risky to the cook (as well as to the diners, I suppose!), so some experience would be preferred. Again, the personal background check is not necessary.

Example: The church is sponsoring an outing. The pastor requests volunteers to drive groups to the site. Is screening needed? Yes, although this should have been thought of ahead of time and planned accordingly. At the very least, the church should have a statement in the Church Policies and Rules that it will not utilize drivers with more than (for example) one ticket in the past three years, one accident in ten years, or any history of DWI.

Example: The youth group is going on a camping trip. The pastor asks for volunteers to accompany them on the weekend excursion. Is screening needed? Yes. There may be a need for certain skills, and the associated risk is greater because the volunteer has overnight access to children—possibly unsupervised, even though there will be other volunteers along.

C. Now, Custom Design an Appropriate Screening System

Given the level and nature of risks involved in any situation, design an appropriate system for screening.

This need not be terribly complex. Let's illustrate:

Illustration: Vehicle Operators
For all persons who plan to drive the church vehicle or their own on behalf of the church, indicate that church policy and appropriate insurance coverage will require the church to review their driving record. A simple questionnaire for all drivers might also be required. This might include name, driver's license number and expiration date, special restrictions if any on the license, accidents and convictions within the past three years, and insurance company and agent.

Illustration: Mission Trip Volunteers
For those involved in work/mission projects, the church might have a standard "Mission Project Questionnaire" (See sample in Appendix.) which might include questions about various skill and task areas that might be involved, including questions related to physical health and limitations, tetanus vaccination status (and others if project is overseas), experience in certain tasks or use of certain equipment, medical insurance, and who to contact in emergencies.

Illustratration: Mom's Morning-Out Volunteers
For those involved as volunteers in a formal day-care or mom's morning-out-type program, the screening process should be virtually as thorough as for employees, unless the volunteer is doing nothing but office-related tasks. And since volunteers in such programs may be asked to do a variety of things, some review of knowledge and skill would be important including things like first-aid abilities, handling infants, supervising certain play activities, etc.

D. Develop Protective Systems Beyond Screening

A good volunteer program should not simply depend on screening. For reasons far beyond just legal risks, most volunteer activities should involve at least three other aspects:

1. Orientation and training

Whether the activity is a youth-weekend retreat or cutting down trees for a shut-in or working in a mom's morning-out program, the volunteers should have some orientation/training which will review their tasks, who's in charge, handling emergencies, equipment/supplies needed, insurance factors, etc.

This may be done both by literature and by pre-activity team meetings.

This would include explanations of any church policies that must be followed during the activity such as no persons, including volunteers, being able to leave the campgrounds, or no camp counselor counseling a teenager alone, or no smoking.

2. Supervision and accountability

In any activity, their should be some supervision of volunteers. Of course, in most church activities, the supervisors may themselves be volunteers, but in any event these need to be persons "in charge."

Effective supervision in major activities may mean someone, paid or volunteer, on site who is in charge of the activity or project. In smaller activities, the supervision may not be actually present at all times, but there will still be the responsible person.

Supervision and acceptability also may be informally structured by assuring that in certain types of activities there will always be more than one volunteer present. For example, in working with children in the nursery or a day-care program, the presence of more than one adult in any room or activity with children is highly desirable from many perspectives—handling emergencies, witnesses to events, protection against unfounded charges of neglect or abuse, etc.

3. Post-activity review

One helpful process in any substantial volunteer activity is to engage in at least some post-activity review which might well include notes on volunteers, including special skills or problems which may have developed.

Certainly, if there were any events during the project/activity that may have created some questions, such as injuries, complaints, disputes, accidents, etc., a more thorough report should be made as contemporaneously as possible, including accounts by those present as to what transpired.

E. Other Options for Screening Volunteers in Higher Risk Contexts

Option 1 - Minimal Approach

Some churches implement a minimum safeguard—requiring that volunteers for high risk positions (like working in the day-care) be members of the church for six to twelve months prior to working as a volunteer. While this requirement is better than nothing, most with criminal or dangerous propensities will not reveal such traits to a fellow parishioner while attending Sunday services for six to twelve months. Since a general knowledge of the person is all that is really gained in such a time, this is still an inadequate method for avoiding problems. Using this system may have catastrophic consequences.

Option 2 - Intermediate Approach

A church may go one step further and implement a shortened version of the hiring process, including some of the steps but not all, and reducing the intensity of some of the steps. While this may be satisfactory in some instances, which phases in the process are truly expendable? The requirements eliminated may be just the ones that are most revealing. Further, if the information is shortened, but only for particular low-risk positions, the church may be safe for the short-run, but additional problems may lurk in the future. What happens when this volunteer performs well in the original task and is later moved to a high-risk position? Unless the church sets up a system for volunteers to "re-apply", and all of the pertinent steps are then followed, the church may end up with the fox in the hen house after all.

If the church can clearly discern which positions are of such low risk that only minimal information need be sought before the volunteer is utilized, and thus shortens the process, the church must simultaneously implement a system which requires volunteers to "re-apply" using the longer process if the volunteer later desires to move into another position. This requires good record keeping and a means of assuring that the ball will never be dropped or an exception made in running the lengthier check as needed.

If a shortened paperwork version of the employment process is selected by the church, one way to create the necessary paperwork is to review the permanent hiring paperwork and simply label unnecessary information with N/A (not applicable). This will force the employer to consider the importance of every question before marking it out. Have the applicant complete the rest. Again, remember that if the volunteer later moves to a more risky position, the church must have the previously omitted information filled out.

Sample forms are provided in the Appendix utilizing this intermediate approach in four common areas: vehicle operator, nursery care in the church, children and youth workers, and field trip/mission project activities.

Option 3 - The Maximum Approach

The third option is definitely the most workable of the three. This option does not cut out any of the steps in the standard hiring process, but delegates some of the paperwork and information checking to volunteers. Recognizing that a need exists for volunteers, as well as recognizing that volunteers represent a potentially huge liability to the church, the installation of a system largely run by volunteers and overseen by a permanent employee may be a church's only viable option.

Many of the paperwork tasks (creating a job description, gathering appropriate forms, having paperwork filled out, and running criminal and driver's record checks) can easily be handled by a volunteer. Further, if a single volunteer can be relied on to handle such matters on a longer-term basis, it may be worthwhile to train the volunteer to conduct interviews and check references as well. All paperwork and responses would be recorded and reviewed by permanent church personnel and red flags duly noted and responded to accordingly. A process of this caliber would go a long way in demonstrating a church's "reasonable care" in the hiring of its volunteer work force.

If a church has a large enough volunteer force to constitute a "problem" in processing the volume of paperwork, it obviously has enough volunteer workers to implement a volunteer paper processing system as well. The designated volunteer will require some training, which will be determined by how much of the process he will be responsible for. It is still important to note that a responsible permanent employee must still review all information gathered from the volunteer before any volunteer is used.

P.S. What is a "Volunteer" — *Classification of "volunteers"*

Who is considered a "volunteer"? The courts will look at several factors in determining that a worker truly is a "volunteer". Consider the following.

- Does not expect any compensation for his/her services

- Is motivated by the desire to contribute to the efforts of the church or organization, not by the desire for compensation

- Is not permitted to enjoy the fringe benefits offered to church employees

- Understands that the church is under no obligation to continue accepting his services or to compensate him/her now or in the future for such services

If any of the above criteria has not been met by the volunteers in your organization, they are not really "volunteers", but "employees." The church may find itself obligated to compensate for past services or extend other employee benefits to those individuals. It may be advisable to request that all volunteers sign a statement that they acknowledge their "volunteer" status and further acknowledge that the above listed criteria are understood and will be abided by. Keep the signed statement in the volunteer's employment file.

Further, if the criteria are not met the court or other agency enforcing labor law, will simply re-classify the "volunteer" as an "employee", and will hold the employer/church liable for all employment activities and obligations as if the volunteer were in fact an employee.

Can employees also be considered volunteers?

Under some circumstances, a church employee may also be considered a volunteer. An employee is free to "volunteer" for other church activities so long as:

- he is not compensated for such activities
- there is not pressure from the employer to engage in such activities
- the activity is performed outside of the employee's regular working hours
- preferably, the work being volunteered for is unrelated to the employee's employment with the church.

Can the volunteer be sued for negligence in connection with his servcies to a charitable organization like a church?

Most states protect volunteers from being sued directly for their negligence while functioning as a volunteer.

Can the volunteer be sued for willful or wanton misconduct or for gross negligence?

That varies by state. Some states protect volunteers from suit even if the conduct is willful and wanton or amounts to gross negligence. More commonly, states do not extend the volunteer immunity to this type of behavior. No state extends immunity from suit to the employer (church or religious organizations included) in this situation.

C-4: Note on Independent Contractors (Self-Employed Workers)

I. Church Use of Self-Employed Workers

II. The Law Regarding "Self-Employed" Workers

III. Who is an Independent Contractor?

I. CHURCH USE OF SELF-EMPLOYED WORKERS

Many churches and religious organizations utilize "self-employed" workers, sometimes referred to as "independent contractors" to supplement their permanent staff. The reasons for utilizing these types of workers are varied. Some churches hope to avoid tax record keeping and administration problems. Others seek to avoid hiring liabilities and hassles. Still others find it a simple means to bring on personnel when and where needed, with no future commitment or obligations on the part of the church.

These "independent contractors" include such people as roofers, plumbers, fund-raising consultants, and lawyers. Occasionally churches have tried to squeeze workers like choir directors into this category for the reasons noted above—no social security liability and other reporting limits.

The "self-employed" worker, however, may also inflict injury on others in the course of his employment with the church. If such self-employed workers are deemed by the court to be actually "employees," the church may be held liable for the injury caused. This creates a hiring situation for the church that is just as potentially dangerous as hiring a permanent employee. Therefore, a correspondingly careful analysis of the hiring process utilized for such positions is in order, and the law and certain criteria must be understood before the church is able to make safe, well-informed hiring decisions.

II. THE LAW REGARDING "SELF-EMPLOYED" WORKERS

We have repeatedly noted that under a negligent hiring claim, the court may find an "employer" liable for injury inflicted by an "employee" if the employer did not take "reasonable care" in hiring, screening, or training an employee. And we have noted that an employer is liable under the legal theory of *respondeat superior* for the harms caused by the negligence of employees acting within the course and scope of their employment.

These liabilities, however, are considerably reduced when dealing with an independent contractor rather than an employee. The employer is usually not liable under *respondeat superior* for the negligence of an independent contractor. Nor does the employer have the same duty to check out the risks posed by an indepedent contractor as he would an employee. If the person inflicting the injury is a self-employed worker, there is no usually no obligation on the part of the contractor (church) to check the backgrounds of those so employed.

Of course, if the church actually knows that an independent contractor, a plumber for example, is a serious risk — as, for example, knowing he has a reputation for assaulting persons, and they hire him anyway, then there may be liability.

III. WHO IS AN INDEPEDENT CONTRACTOR?

To avoid liability for the actions of the worker, then, it is important that the worker be defined by the church as "self-employed" rather than as an "employee." But, the "self-employed" label placed upon the worker *by the employer* is not determinative in deciding whether a court of law will also consider the worker "self-employed". The court may determine otherwise, and thus impose an obligation or liability upon an employer. The law, in fact, utilizes a much more apparent system for determining the classification of workers—it looks at the actual relationship between the worker and the employer.

When the court analyzes the relationship between the worker and the employer, it is seeking to determine the amount of "control" the employer exercises over the worker. If the employer dictates much of the activities of the worker, the worker is effectively functioning as an "employee" and will be considered as such. In the eyes of the court, if it acts like a duck, it is a duck.

A. Standards for Analyzing the Proper Employee Classification

In determining the amount of control exercised by the employer, and thus the status of the "self-employed" worker versus an "employee", a number of questions can be asked. The answers should reveal a pattern and will give the church some insight into the types of information a court will probably consider in weighing the amount of control involved. If the answers to many of the following questions are "yes", the courts will most likely find the worker to be an "employee".

B. "Employee" Characteristics:

* Does the church dictate when the worker will perform his/her tasks?

* Does the church require on-going training or the worker's attendance at certain seminars or classes?

* Does the church have an on-going program for developing the worker's skills or training?

* Must the worker take advantage of classes or training given for the benefit of permanent workers?

* Does the employer evaluate the worker's individual performance, give reviews, or provide feedback as would be given a permanent employee?

* Does the employer maintain close supervision over the methods or content of the work?

* Does the employer, rather than the worker, make decisions such as adding help for the project or determining the best way to complete a project?

* Can the employer make crew hiring and firing decisions on the site?

* Does the employer, rather than the worker, make decisions regarding the working of overtime to ensure that deadlines are met?

* Does the employer dictate the method the worker follows, rather than relying on the expertise and advise of the worker?

* Is the employer the sole source of work for the worker?

- Does the employer prohibit the worker from obtaining work from others?

- Does the employer compensate the worker on an hourly basis rather than on a per job basis or contract basis?

- Does the employer prohibit the worker from advertising his/her services or promoting his/her business outside the church?

The above questions, while not totally inclusive, indicate the types of factors that a court could consider in evaluating an employer/employee relationship. A "yes" on one or two of the questions may not be conclusive, but an overriding number of "yes" answers clearly indicates a pattern of behavior between the parties and may be interpreted as reflecting an employer/employee relationship.

Section D: Federal Statutory Overview

A. Title VII, Civil Rights Act of 1964
B. Equal Pay Act of 1963
C. Family and Medical Leave Act of 1993
D. Fair Labor Standards Act (FLSA) 1938
E. Age Discrimination In Employment Act (1967)
F. Americans With Disabilities Act of 1990
G. Immigration Reform And Control Act of 1986

Supplement: North Carolina Statutes

A. Handicapped Persons Protection Act
B. Wage And Hour Act
C. Equal Employment Practices Act
D. Blacklisting Employees
E. Discrimination Against Any Person Possessing Sickle Cell Trait Or Hemoglobin C Trait
F. Confidentiality Of Records
G. Laboratory Tests For AIDS Virus Infection
H. Discrimination Against Military Personnel
I. National Guard Reemployment Rights
J. Department of Labor Regulation Barring Discrimination Against Persons for Use ofLawful Product
K. Day Care Employee Requirements
L. Immunity From Civil Liability For Volunteers

INTRODUCTION

This section is not an attempt to provide an exhaustive analysis of a growing and complex area of the law. Instead, we seek here to familiarize the reader with the regulations that may affect church hiring decisions.

We have attempted to lay out the federal law in a consistent and user friendly fashion, highlighting important facts especially as they relate to the application of the law to churches.

However, the legal arena is changing daily. Even professionals in the field of employment law find it difficult to second guess where the law or the legislature will make its next turn. For this reason it is always a good practice to consult an attorney if a questionable situation arises. An attorney will be able to offer the most up to date information and professional advice.

Many states create legislation designed to expand or supplement the federal regulation in a specific area. In the employment arena there is a vast array of such state law. Before an employer can feel truly confident in his employment practices, the applicability of state laws must be known.

If a conflict occurs between the coverage offered under the state and federal laws, two things may occur. First, the state may seek to apply its own laws and the plaintiff will be forced to bring his action in the federal court system in order to take advantage of the federal law. Second, the state may have accommodated such a conflict by requiring the state to refuse to hear cases which have been filed in the federal court system. In the event the state law is more expansive than the federal law, the plaintiff may file in state court and take advantage of the state law.

The statutory context is especially critical in any discrimination claim. A church as a private entity, is not subject to constitutionally-based limits on permissible discrimination such as contained in the equal protection clause of the fourteenth amendment. Private employers, including churches, may engage in all different types of preferential hiring. Their rights to do so are only limited to the extent there is a valid law—federal, state or local—which bars or limits that right. Therefore, it is very important to be aware of stautory developments.

Federal Statutory Applicability to Churches

Church Type (by # of employees)	Civil Rights Act	American with Disabilities Act	Age Discrimination in Employment	Fair Labor Standards Act	Equal Pay Act	Immigration Reform and Control Act	Family Leave Act
Small Church (Less than 15 employees)	No	No	No	Yes, if church is "employer" and engaged in commerce	Yes, for all "employees" and "enterprises"	Yes, if church is an "employer"	No
Medium Church (15-19 employees)	Yes, if engaged in business or affecting commerce. Religious organizations are exempt from prohibition on religious discrimination	Yes, but only if it is a business affecting commerce.	No	Same as Above	Same as Above	Same as Above	No
Large Church (20+ employees)	Same as Above	Same as Above	Yes, but only if it is engaged in an industry affecting commerce.	Same as Above	Same as Above	Same as Above	No / Yes if -- 50+ employees and engaged in business affecting commerce

A. TITLE VII, CIVIL RIGHTS ACT OF 1964

I. KEY TEXT

"it shall be unlawful employment practice for an employer (1) to fail or refuse to hire or to discharge any individual, or otherwise to discriminate against any individual with respect to his compensation, terms, conditions, or privileges of employment, because of such individual's race, color, religion, sex, or national origin; or (2) to limit, segregate, or classify his employees or applicants for employment in any way which would deprive or tend to deprive any individual of employment opportunity or otherwise adversely affect his status as an employee, because of such individual's race, color, religion, sex or national origin." 42 U.S.C. §§2000e et. Seq.

Later amended to include "pregnancy, childbirth or related medical conditions. . . ."

Courts have also prohibited "sexual harassment" under Title VII.

II. JURISDICTIONAL TRIGGERS

- Employers with 15+ employees working full time for 20 calendar weeks AND

- Whose business affects commerce OR who is engaged in a business activity

III. CHURCH APPLICABILITY

- most churches are not covered by the act because they do not "affect commerce" or are not "engaged in business"

- further, the act specifically exempts "religious organizations" from liability for religious discrimination

- the exemption for "religious organizations" from religious discrimination allows a church to discriminate based on religion in ANY area of the church (school, staff, church help, janitorial, etc.)

- the term "religious organization" includes churches, schools, church-run retirement homes, church headquarters, and non-profit religious organizations (but, some courts have interpreted it to include only churches)

- employment decisions involving the clergy are not covered by federal anti-discrimination laws

Further exemptions:

- a sincerely held religious belief may justify a religious organization's discriminatory practices

- any employer may also discriminate based on a Bona Fide Occupational Qualification (BFOQ)

- a BFOQ will never justify discrimination based on race or color

- A BFOQ is defined as a qualification "reasonably necessary to the operation of the business"

- an employee's ability to perform the essential functions of the job must depend on the discriminatory characteristic

- any employer may also justify a discriminatory practice based on the Business Necessity Doctrine

IV. RECORD KEEPING REQUIREMENTS:

- any employment or personnel records must be kept for six months from the date of making the record

- this requirement is not applicable to pre-employment forms (such as applications) for seasonal or temporary positions

V. ANALYSIS

The Civil Rights Act of 1964, particularly Title VII, is the most expansive and far reaching of the acts prohibiting discrimination in employment. The Act lists several factors which employers are prohibited from using in making hiring, promotion, termination, or other employment decisions. The list of factors, or "protected classes", has been expanded over time and may continue to be. At this point, homosexuals and transsexuals are not protected classes, though more and more states and municipalities are passing laws to protect them.

Who is covered?

The act does not cover all employers. There are two criteria an employer must meet to be included, and if either is not met, the employer is not covered and is, then, not legally barred from basing employment decisions on these otherwise discriminatory factors. The employer must employ 15 or more employees, and only those that work 20 calendar weeks in a year will be counted. Second, the employer must "affect commerce" or be engaged in a "business activity".

The second criteria, "affecting commerce" or engaged in a "business activity", can be slippery to define. Although non-profits are generally not considered to be engaged in commerce, and, thus, do not "affect commerce", the Commerce Clause of the United States Constitution has been so broadly interpreted that it now reaches almost any type of activity. If the activities of churches and non-profit organizations were to be viewed in this light, they would meet the second criteria.

As a general rule, whether or not an organization is "affecting commerce" is looked at on a case by case basis. The court will consider the size, reach, and commercial applicability of the organization and activity in question.

Religious organization exemption for religious discrimination

"Religious organizations" are specifically exempted for any discrimination based on religion. This means that even if a religious organization meets the above criteria and is covered under the Act, it will still be allowed to consider religion in making hiring decisions.

The term "religious organization" has generally included churches, schools, church-run retirement homes, church headquarters, and non-profit religious organizations. However, some courts have construed "religious organization" to include only churches. While this is a minority view now, if this view were ever adopted by the Supreme Court, only churches would be allowed to systematically base employment decisions on religion.

Church exemption in hiring clergy

When hiring its clergy, churches may discriminate based on many otherwise prohibited factors. So far the courts have considered the application of anti-discrimination laws to the clergy to be barred by the First amendment. A question arises, however, when the court tries to define "clergy".

There are two tests which have been used by the court to determine if a position is properly labeled as "clergy." The Functional Test seeks to determine if the position is truly related to a spiritual mission, while the Ordination Test looks strictly at whether the person has actually been ordained. The theory behind the use of the Ordination Test is that no church would ordain a minister simply to avoid discrimination laws.

Religious organization's discrimination based on religious tenet:

If a religious organization can show that it has a sincerely held religious belief which dictates the use of prohibited factors in its hiring decisions, it may be allowed to discriminate based on those factors. These religious beliefs are generally derived from a sacred text or religious or spiritual source which is central to the practice of that religion.

Other justifications for discriminatory practices

If an organization found that the court did not consider it a "religious organization", there is another way the organization could continue to consider religion and otherwise discriminatory factors in making employment decisions. The use of such factors could be justified by Bona Fide Occupational Qualifications (BFOQ's). This is a qualification that is "reasonably necessary to the operation of the business". If a particular position reasonably requires a particular gender, for example, the employer could base that hiring decision on gender--an otherwise prohibited practice.

An organization could also justify its discriminatory practices by utilizing the Business Necessity Doctrine. If the employer has a neutral policy or practice that can be justified by a legitimate business necessity, the employer may consider otherwise discriminatory factors in its hiring decisions.

B. EQUAL PAY ACT OF 1963

I. TEXT

"no employer . . . Shall discriminate . . . Between employees on the basis of sex for equal work on jobs the performance of which requires equal skill, effort and responsibility, and which are performed under similar working conditions, except where such payment is made pursuant to (i) a seniority system; (ii) a merit system; (iii) a system which measures earnings by quantity or quality of production; or (iv) a differential based on any other factor other than sex . . . ." 29 U.S.C. §206(d)(1).

II. JURISDICTION

- applies to all "enterprises"

- applies to all enterprise "employees"

III. CHURCH APPLICABILITY

- applicable to all church-related schools and preschools

- no special exemptions for religious organizations or churches

- "ministers" are exempt, as they are not considered "employees"

IV. ANALYSIS

The Equal Pay Act was passed in 1963 as an amendment to the Fair Labor Standards Act. This act specifically prohibits the paying of varying wage rates due to gender.

Who is covered?

The courts have determined that the first criteria for coverage under the Equal Pay Act is that the institution be an "enterprise". Enterprise, as used in the Act, includes any activities performed by any person or persons for a business purpose. This wide reading specifically encompasses all secular and religious preschools, elementary or secondary schools, and institutions of higher education.

The second requirement in determining the applicability of the Act is that the claimant be an "employee". Since ministers are often not considered "employees", churches have attempted to avoid the act by labeling a teacher a "minister".

The courtS, however, have looked beyond the label of the position to determine if, in fact, the person is a minister versus an "employee". The court considers such criteria as: sacerdotal functions performed, membership in a religious order, and service in positions of ministerial leadership within the church. The court has been consistent in applying the Act stringently. An institution would have little chance in avoiding the Act for almost any school related employee.

Consequences of a violation:

If it is determined that the Equal Pay Act has been violated, the institution may not decrease the pay of other workers in order to align the wages. The underpaid employee's wage must be raised to conform to that of others.

C. FAMILY AND MEDICAL LEAVE ACT OF 1993

I. TEXT

". . . the birth of a son or daughter of the employee and in order to care for that son or daughter. . . adoption or foster care placement in the employee's home. . . Care of a spouse, son, daughter or parent if one of these persons has a "serious health condition". . . or a serious health condition "that makes the employee unable to perform the functions of the position of such employee"...entitles an eligible employee to 12 weeks of unpaid leave. . . ."

II. JURISDICTION

- employers with 50+ "eligible" employees

- AND who are also "engaged in" or "affecting commerce"

III. CHURCH APPLICABILITY

- most churches do not employee 50+ employees and, thus, are exempt

- most local churches are probably not "engaged in" or "affecting" commerce

- operating a school or college will qualify as "affecting commerce"

- interstate circulation of brochures or paraphernalia may constitute "affecting commerce"

IV. ANALYSIS

Who is covered?

The first criteria is that the employer have 50 or more eligible employees. To be considered an "eligible" employee under the Act, one must have been employed by that employer for at least 12 months. Also, the employee must have worked at least 1,250 hours during the prior twelve month period.

The second criteria is that the employer be "affecting commerce". Although this is a very recent Act and cases will need to be heard before the reach of this requirement can be determined, it is not likely that "affecting commerce" will be read as broadly under this act as it is under others.

How does the act work?

Once an employee takes leave under the Act, the employer must hold that position open for the employee, or offer the employee a comparable position with the same pay and benefits when he returns to work. During the leave time, the employer must also continue to offer coverage under the company's medical program, but the company may recover costs for this benefit if the employee fails to return to work.

The employee has obligations under the Act as well. The employee must, when practicable, give thirty-day notice of expected leave (for example, the expected birth date of a child or pre-scheduled medical procedures). Also, the employee must attempt to accommodate the employer by scheduling, when possible, the leave in the least disruptive manner.

The employee may also be required to present "certification" of a reason for the leave, and the employee may later be required to cooperate in obtaining a second opinion. The employee must also keep the employer abreast of changes regarding a scheduled return date.

If an employer employs both husband and wife, the employer is not required to offer the twelve-week leave to both parties to attend to the same emergency or occurrence.

If sick pay or vacation pay is available, an employer may require that the employee deplete this pay before taking the remaining time as unpaid.

Possible exemptions:

There are specific exemptions for very highly paid employees, but few religious institutions need worry about these. "Highly compensated" employees need not be offered their original positions, though most organizations would want to be particularly accommodating of these valued employees.

Other considerations:

As with all other policies and procedures, the employer must be careful to apply medical leave benefits uniformly. If one employee is allowed a longer leave than the Act requires, other employees must enjoy the same benefit, regardless of whether or not the institution is covered by this Act.

D. FAIR LABOR STANDARDS ACT (FLSA) (1938)

I. TEXT

"the act . . . protects employees from substandard wages and excessive working hours . . . requires equal pay for equal work . . . and restricts the employment of underage children. . . ."

II. JURISDICTION

- enterprises "engaged in commerce" or in the "production of goods for commerce"

- AND the act covers only "employers"

- a plaintiff may sue either or both the employer and the individual employee

III. CHURCH APPLICABILITY

- most churches and religious organizations do not consider themselves "engaged in commerce", but for purposes of this Act the courts have read "commerce" very broadly and the act is now applied to all but the smallest churches and organizations

- the Act expressly covers educational facilities, and courts have defined the act to cover religious schools

- this Act can apply to the commercial aspects of a religious organization while exempting the religious activities

- a particular position within a religious organization may be exempt on first amendment grounds if it involves an employee directly involved with the religious ministries of the church, such as the minister

- employees who exercise discretion (administrators, professionals, and executives) are considered "exempt" employees for purposes of this act

IV. ANALYSIS

Who is covered?

The first requirement for coverage under this Act is that the organization be an "enterprise". The act defines enterprise as "the related activities performed...by any person or persons for a common business purpose." The Act was later amended to specifically include schools, regardless of whether or not they were profit or non-profit, secular or religious, or private or public. The operation of any school is now deemed to be for a common business purpose, and thus covered by the Act.

The act requires not only that the institution be an "enterprise", but that it be "engaged in commerce" or "in the production of goods for commerce". The act has defined two circumstances in which these criteria are met:

(1) The employees produce goods or are engaged in commerce by handling, selling, or otherwise working on goods. . . AND gross volume of sales made or business done is not less than $500,000.

(2) The enterprise is engaged in the operation of a preschool, elementary or secondary school, or an institution of higher education.

If a non-profit tax-exempt organization is not performing functions for a "business purpose", and is not performing other unrelated business income activities, any activities in furtherance of the religious purpose should be free from regulation under the Act. However, in actuality, "business purpose" has been very broadly read and almost any activity can now be used to place a religious organization under the umbrella of this act. Only the smallest, most local and isolated churches are still outside the realm of this Act.

Volunteers are never covered under the Act, as they are not "employees". It is important for a church to note that ANY compensation expected by the volunteer could be considered income for services rendered, and may negate the volunteer's status as a "volunteer". He will then be considered an "employee", and will be covered by the act.

Who is exempt?

Ministers are seldom considered "employees", and are, thus, usually exempt from the Act. Executive, administrative, professional, and outside sales employee exemptions are also available.

- "Executive" includes those with management or director responsibilities that receive $130/week or more.

- "Administrative" personnel perform the support or office functions of the organization or executive personnel, and receive a salary of $130/week or more.

- "Professional" employees hold a degree or specialized knowledge and receive $150/week or more, and this category specifically includes teachers.

If an employee falls within any of the exempt categories, the FLSA will not apply to them, though the rest of the employees in the organization may still be covered.

Applicable state law:

Most states have also addressed this area of employment law. For a complete determination of the laws affecting your organization, please consult your state laws.

E. AGE DISCRIMINATION IN EMPLOYMENT ACT (1967)

I. TEXT

"It is unlawful for an employer . . . to refuse to hire . . . to discharge . . . to limit, segregate, or classify their employees . . . or otherwise adversely affect . . . [the] status as an employee because of such individual's age . . . ."

II. JURISDICTION

- employers of 20+ eligible employees, AND

- who are "engaged in an industry affecting commerce"

III. CHURCH APPLICABILITY

- churches are not specifically exempt

- clergy are not covered, though the organization may still be

- certain tenured employees of higher education may be exempt, but other employees will still be covered if the employer falls within the above criteria

- certain executives in high positions may also be exempt, but again, other employees will be covered if the requirements above are met

- mandatory retirement, even in churches, is not allowed

- mandatory retirement may be allowed for those exempt under the tenured employee, executives in high positions, or ministerial exemptions

IV. RECORD KEEPING REQUIREMENTS

The Act requires that the following records be maintained in order to track and verify that the employer is complying with the Act.

- all job applications must be kept for 1 year
- payroll information must be kept for 3 years
- personnel records must be kept for 1 year
- help wanted ads, notices, training opportunities, promotional information, and court records must be kept for 1 year

V. ANALYSIS

This Act specifically addresses age discrimination against any employee 40 years of age or older. The Act originally protected employees up to the age of 65, but this cap has since been removed.

Who is covered?

This Act only applies to employers who meet two criteria. First, the employer must employ 20 or more employees who work 20 or more weeks in a calendar year. Second, the employer must be engaged in an industry affecting commerce. Most churches do not employ the necessary 20 employees, and most are not engaged in a business affecting commerce. Therefore, in most cases, churches are not covered by this Act.

Is the Act applicable to churches?

Churches are not exempt from the Act. If the church meets the above two requirements it will be expected to comply with the anti-age discrimination laws.

The clergy, however, are not regulated by federal employment laws. To date, the courts have been unwilling to hear cases brought by the clergy against the church. Because the clergy are so inextricably entwined in the running of the church and the practice of its religion, it would be difficult for the court to discern between a decision based on discriminatory grounds or one based on the spiritual needs of the church. The court's reluctance to hear such cases could change in the future.

The church is in a far different position with non-clergy employees. The court has not created a general exemption for religious employers since employment issues such as age discrimination do not generally infringe upon an institution's religious convictions.

Further, religious organizations could discriminate based on age if it could be shown that the discriminatory practice was based on a religious tenet.

Mandatory retirement:

Although forcing an employee to retire is prohibited by this Act, it is permitted for employees over the age of 70 in certain situations. Tenured employees of higher education institutions may be forced to retire, as well as top level executive whose retirement benefits would exceed a set minimum level. Clergy may also be forced to retire, since, as stated above, this Act does not protect them. Factors established by the church in selecting the appropriate clergy for the church may also incorporate age as a determinate.

Possible exemptions:

If an employer (either religious or secular) can establish that age is a bona fide occupational qualification (BFOQ), it may discriminate based upon it.

F. AMERICANS WITH DISABILITIES ACT OF 1990 (ADA)

I. TEXT

To prohibit "unfair and unnecessary discrimination" and to provide "people with disabilities the opportunity to compete on an equal basis and to pursue those opportunities for which our free society is justifiably famous. . . ." 42 USCS §§ 12101 et seq.

"Disability" is herein defined as "physical or mental impairment, history of impairment, or what others regard to be an impairment."

II. JURISDICTION

- employers with 15 or more employees working 20 weeks in a calendar year

- AND whose business is "affecting commerce"

III. APPLICABILITY TO CHURCHES

- there is no general exemption for religious organizations or churches

- most churches, however, are not covered because they are not "affecting commerce"

- further, a religious organization could be exempt if its discriminatory practice is based on a religious tenet

IV. ANALYSIS

This Act was enacted in 1990 and is possibly the most extensive piece of federal legislation since the Civil Rights Act. The Act received mixed reactions from businesses, who were frightened that the accommodations required of them in accommodating disabled workers would be too burdensome.

Who is covered?

The jurisdiction of this Act mirrors that of Title VII of the Civil Rights Act. There are two requirements that must be met before an employer will be covered. First, the employer must employ fifteen or more employees for twenty weeks in a calendar year. Second, the business must be "affecting commerce".

This is a fairly new act, so it has yet to be determined how broadly the court will define "affecting commerce". Commerce has been very broadly read in applying certain civil rights and child labor laws, but less broadly interpreted in other contexts. One would anticipate that "affecting commerce" will be applied in its traditional sense here.

Most churches are not "engaged in a business" and do not "affect commerce", although a religious organization's commercial enterprises or extensive inter-state outreach programs could move it into this category. The employer would also have to meet the 15 employee hurdle to be included.

Is the act applicable to churches?

The Act is generally applicable to all churches and religious organizations, assuming they meet the above listed criteria. In certain circumstances, however, the church can avoid coverage.

First, the selection and hiring of clergy in the church is never covered by the Act. The church is protected by the first amendment from regulation and interference regarding its ministerial decisions.

Second, a religious tenet may be established to justify a decision in certain cases. A religious tenet is a sincerely held religious belief based on a sacred text or religious or spiritual source which is central to the practice of that religion. Most conceivably this could come into play if the "disabled" person was a homosexual with AIDS applying with a church. If the church had a religious tenet regarding homosexuality and regularly required all employees to agree to uphold and abide by its religious doctrines, a conflict would occur.

It is difficult to say what the outcome of such a situation would be. Such a case has not yet arisen. However, the church has a strong position in claiming that the practice of its religion would be infringed upon by forcing the church to hire such individuals.

Third, a bona fide occupational qualification (BFOQ) can be used to justify a hiring decision based on a disability. The BFOQ must, however, relate to the applicant's ability to perform the essential functions of the position. A BFOQ can be established by either a religious or secular employer.

What constitutes an "impairment":

The first type of impairment exists if a physical or mental impairment substantially limits one or more major life activities. These life activities include seeing, hearing, speaking, breathing, and walking.

The second category of impairment is a history of such impairment. Under this grouping recovering alcoholics or drug abusers are protected from discriminatory hiring practices. Active users are not included.

The third category of impairment covers those regarded by others as having a disability. These people are covered even if they do not, in fact, have such a disability. If sexual preference were ever to be regarded as a protected disability, it would fall within this category (though this is not the case at this time).

The use of medical exams:

The proper use of medical exams is critical, and several points must be made regarding them. First, the medical exam must be job related. Second, the medical exam may only be utilized to determine whether or not the applicant is able to perform job-related functions, or to create a confidential medical record. Third, the exam may only be conducted post-offer. And, fourth, if a medical exam is required, it must be required of all employees, not just the disabled. Drug testing is not considered a "medical" exam, and is, therefore, not covered by the above criteria.

What are the covered employer's obligations?

The employer must make "reasonable accommodations" to enable the disabled employee to perform the job. "Reasonable accommodation" has been defined to include: the modification of facilities, the restructuring of a job, specific training, and modification of work schedules.

The employer will not be forced to make such "reasonable accommodations" if it will impose an "undue hardship" upon the business. "Undue hardship" can be determined using several different factors, including: cost of the accommodation, the financial resources of the business, and the nature of the operations of the business. This reflects the legislature's recognition that certain industries and sectors (including churches) often do not have funds available for such accommodations.

G. IMMIGRATION REFORM AND CONTROL ACT OF 1986

I. TEXT

". . . prohibits employers from knowingly hiring, recruiting, or referring for a fee any person not authorized to work in the United States . . . to continue to employ a person who has become unauthorized to work . . . or using a contract . . . to obtain the labor of an unauthorized alien." 8 U.S.C. § 1324a et seq.

II. JURISDICTION

- all "employers" regardless of size

III. APPLICABILITY TO CHURCHES

- yes; however, volunteers are never considered employees and ministers are generally not, so the church would not be deemed an "employer" for these workers under this Act

- religious organizations must be careful to properly utilize the required I-9 form, since random checks are made by the INS and fines can reach up to $10,000 per violation

IV. ANALYSIS

The Act was designed to eliminate the employment of illegal aliens in this country. For this reason, all employers are covered, regardless of size.

This Acts\ forces the employer to verify the worker's status by obtaining a completed I-9 form from each applicant before he is hired.

Procedural outline:

The I-9 form must be filled out by each and every employee. If there is any question as to the minister's status as an "employee" versus an "independent contractor", have one on file for him as well.

The required I-9 form is available from the Immigration and Naturalization Service (INS). The employer may make copies for future use, but must be sure to copy and retain the instructions (contained on the back of the form) along with the applicant portion.

The instructions on the back of the form clearly outline how the form is to be filled out. The applicant is asked to produce two pieces of acceptable identification (what is considered acceptable is listed on the form), fill out some simple information (birth date, address, etc.), sign the form, and have the employer verify the identification produced by the applicant and sign accordingly.

Record keeping:

The I-9 form must be filed separately from the rest of the employment information. Since the date of birth is contained on the I-9 form and information on age cannot be considered in employment decisions, holding the I-9 form with the employee's personnel records would be highly suspect if a claim were ever made.

The completed I-9 form must be retained for three years after the date of hire or one year after employment ends, whichever is later.

Enforcement:

The INS makes unannounced audits of random employer's I-9 forms. Even if the employer has not hired any illegal aliens, the employer will still be fined (up to $10,000 per form) for any missing or incomplete I-9 forms.

SUPPLEMENT: NORTH CAROLINA STATUTES

A. HANDICAPPED PERSONS PROTECTION ACT

I. TEXT

"to encourage and enable all handicapped people to participate fully to the maximum extent of their capabilities in...social and economic life...employment...public accommodation and public services..." NCGS § 168a et seq.

Companion Act to the federal Americans with Disabilities Act (ADA)

II. JURISDICTION

Who is covered?

- employers with 15+ full-time employees
- farm workers and domestic help do not count towards the 15 employee requirement if they are the employer's only employees

Who is exempt?

- there is no exemption for religious organizations

III. DIFFERENCES BETWEEN THIS ACT AND THE ADA:

- this Act allows injunctive and declaratory relief only; the ADA allows equitable relief as well

- the Act clearly states that "physical and mental impairment" does not include sexual preferences

- this Act measures "undue hardship" differently than the subjective analysis used under the ADA; North Carolina considers any expense greater than 5% of the employee's salary to be an undue burden on the employer

- after an employer attempts a "reasonable accommodation" he may use the disability as a factor in an employment decision if he can show: an inability to perform duties based on the same standards applied to other workers, or creation of an unreasonable risk to the disabled individual or to others

B. NORTH CAROLINA WAGE AND HOUR ACT

I. TEXT

"wage levels of employees, payment of earned wages, and the well-being of minors are subjects of concern requiring legislation to promote the general welfare of the people of the state..." NCGS § 95-25.1 et seq.

Companion Act to the federal Fair Labor Standards Act (FLSA)

II. JURISDICTION

Who is covered?

- anyone not covered by the FLSA

III. DIFFERENCES BETWEEN THIS ACT AND THE FLSA:

- this Act defines "overtime" as hours worked over 45 per week; FLSA uses 40 hours per week

- seasonal and church exemptions (above)

IV. APPLICABILITY TO CHURCHES

- churches are not exempt

- under the FLSA churches are at times exempt because they do not "affect commerce"; these exempt organizations would be covered under the NC Act

- ministers are still exempt on first amendment grounds

- seasonal non-profit or religious organizational conference centers are specifically exempt

- volunteers in a religious or non-profit organization are exempt (since volunteers are not employees)

C. N. C. EQUAL EMPLOYMENT PRACTICES ACT

I. TEXT

"it is the public policy...To protect and safeguard the right...Of all persons to seek, obtain and hold employment without discrimination...on account of race, religion, color, national origin, age, sex or handicap..." NCGS § 143-422.1

Companion Act to the federal Civil Rights Act.

II. COVERAGE

- anyone regularly employing 15 or more employees

III. DIFFERENCES BETWEEN THIS ACT AND THE FEDERAL ACT:

- this Act is a "public policy" act only; it does not mandate that employers comply, but merely states that "it is the public policy of this state..."

IV. APPLICABILITY TO CHURCHES

- no one is specifically exempt, but the first amendment still protects clergy from such regulation

- also, a religious tenet or a BFOQ could still justify discrimination based on one of these factors

D. BLACKLISTING EMPLOYEES

I. TEXT

It is unlawful to "prevent or attempt to prevent...Discharged employees from obtaining employment" NCGS § 14-355.

II. COVERAGE

- all employers are covered, without exception

- this Act does not apply to written statements of why the employee was discharged if the information is relayed to a prospective employer (i.e., during a reference check)

- under this Act, both or either the employer or an individual employee may be sued

E. DISCRIMINATION AGAINST ANY PERSON POSSESSING SICKLE CELL TRAIT OR HEMOGLOBIN C TRAIT

I. TEXT

It is unlawful "to deny or refuse...Or discharge any person from employment on account of the fact such person possesses sickle cell trait or hemoglobin c trait." NCGS § 95-28.1

II. COVERAGE

- all persons, firms, corporations, unincorporated associations, state agencies, local governments, or any public or private entity

- obviously, churches and religious organizations are included

- a direct conflict would occur if a religious organization discriminated based on either of these factors because of a religious tenet--no case has come to light in this regard

F. CONFIDENTIALITY OF RECORDS

I. TEXT

"all records...That identify a person who has AIDS...Shall be strictly confidential" NCGS § 130a-143

II. COVERAGE

- this applies to all employers, even churches

G. LABORATORY TESTS FOR AIDS VIRUS INFECTION

I. TEXT

- outlined under NCGS § 130A-148(i), this Act prohibits employers from conducting AIDS tests to determine an applicant's suitability for continued employment

- this Act further states that it is "unlawful to discriminate against persons with AIDS"

H. DISCRIMINATION AGAINST MILITARY PERSONNEL

I. TEXT

This act ensures that "no discrimination against military personnel is practiced by any business, persons..." NCGS § 127b, article 2

The act prohibits discrimination due to an employee's membership in the service

II. COVERAGE

- all employers are included under this Act

I. NATIONAL GUARD REEMPLOYMENT RIGHTS

I. PROVISIONS

- NCGS § 127A-201 et seq. provides that after an honorable release from service with the North Carolina National Guard, qualified employees must be returned to their former positions or positions of like seniority, status, and salary.

- The employer will not have to restore the employee to a position if circumstances at that time make the restoration unreasonable.

- If the employee is no longer "qualified," the employee must be placed in another position for which he is qualified unless the circumstances at that time make such a move unreasonable.

J. LABOR DEPT. REGULATION BARRING DISCRIMINATION AGAINST PERSONS FOR USE OF LAWFUL PRODUCT

I. TEXT

- "discrimination against persons for lawful use of lawful products during nonworking hours prohibited." NCGS § 95-28.2.

- "employers" covered here include all types of public employers, corporations, quasi-corporations, and private employers with three or more employees. There is no specific exemption for religious employers.

K. DAY-CARE EMPLOYEE REQUIREMENTS

I. TEXT

"each child day care facility shall be under the direction or supervision of a literate person at least 21 years of age. All staff counted in determining the required staff-child ratio shall be at least 16 years of age, provided that persons younger than 18 years of age work under the direct supervision of a literate staff person who is at least 21 years of age. No person shall be an operator of nor be employed in a child day care facility who has been convicted of a crime involving child neglect child abuse, or moral turpitude, or who is an habitually excessive user of alcohol or who illegally uses narcotic or other impairing drugs, or who is mentally or emotionally impaired to an extent that may be injurious to children.

II. COVERAGE

Though many day-care regulations are waived for religious institutions, this one has been specifically applied to them.

L. IMMUNITY FROM CIVIL LIABILITY FOR VOLUNTEERS

I. TEXT

"a volunteer who performs services for a charitable organization is not liable in civil damages for any acts or omissions resulting in any injury, death, or loss to person or property arising from volunteer services rendered if:...." NCGS § 1-539.10

II. CONDITIONS FOR IMMUNITY

A. The volunteer was acting in good faith.

B. Services rendered were reasonable under the circumstances.

C. The acts or omissions did not amount to gross negligence, wanton conduct, or intentional wrongdoing.

D. The acts or omissions did not occur while the volunteer was operating or responsible for the operation of a motor vehicle.

E. Further, the charitable organization or volunteer, if either has liability insurance, will be deemed to have waived their immunity to the extent of that insurance. This means that the insured will have to reimburse the victim for that injury to the limit of its coverage. Expenses over that amount will not be recoverable from either the organization or volunteer.

NOTES

Appendix

I. Forms

COMMENTS ON FORMS

I. General Application

This form, as the title indicates, is a "general" form which seeks to obtain a broad range of information about the applicant. For a specific task, such as secretary, choir director, day-care worker, custodian, etc., the church should, as noted in Section B, develop a Supplemental Application designed to reflect the needs in that specific position.

II. Employee Handbook Disclosure Form

If the church has an employee handbook, then every applicant should sign this form indicating they understand the limited scope of the Handbook's provisions. The Handbook itself should also contain a similar provision about its non-contractual character.

III. "At-Will" Employee Status Declaration

This statement is intended to make clear that notwithstanding any other representations, the employment relationship is "at-will" which means the employee may be terminated at any time for any reason. Of course, if a church wishes to establish some other relationship with a greater commitment to employment, such as annually renewable, then it is free to do so, but most churches do not hire by such formal contract.

IV. Interview Form

This, again, is a generic interview form which would be used by the person or committee interviewing applicants. As with the generic Application, it would need to be supplemented with specific inquiries related to the specific job being considered, as for example in the Child-Care Interview Supplement which follows.

V. Child-Care Interview Supplement

This interview supplement suggests the sort of questions and discussion which ought to take place in the context of the hiring of Day-Care personnel. It is intended to supplement the more general Interview Form.

VI. Nursery Volunteer Worker Registration Form

This form is an attempt to provide a basic information gathering process for the typical Sunday morning-type nursery worker at the church. It is an attempt to balance the need for some scrutiny of those who work with children—both for competence and risk avoidance—and the fact that a cumbersome process will simply drive away volunteers who are offended. This minimal screening should NOT be used for more intensive child-care situations such as a Day-Care program. It assumes in a typical church that there are at least two, and usually more, adults present.

The form is intended to provide information as to special skills and emergency information, as well as surface risk factors.

We have used the terminology "registration form" or "information form" on this and the next several forms in order to lower the frustration or bad feelings that may result if volunteers were asked to "apply" to be more formally screened.

VII. Volunteer Driver Registration Form

Because vehicle operation is a major source of risk and potential liability, this form is intended to provide not only helpful skill information, and emergency information, but to raise issues of unreasonable risks because of driver's prior record.

VIII. Work Project/Mission Trip Volunteer Registration Form

Mission trips and work projects are also areas where it is important that those who participate have the needed skills and do not pose unreasonable risks given the nature of the activities. This form is a sort of minimal screening and information gathering device.

IX. Children's And Youth Ministry Volunteer Information Form

Any activity with children and youth involves risk related both to lack of skills as well as character. This form is intended to provide basic screening and skills information for the church on those who are going to be involved in these activities. This is NOT intended as an adequate screening for full-time staff persons in the church or day care, but the occasional volunteer working in a multiple staff situation.

X. Reference Release Form

This form should be completed by applicants, and may be helpful in obtaining more full disclosure from references.

XI. Reference Check Form

This form is a guide for discussing the applicant with the references the applicant has provided and other references identified. It is generic in form and may need to be supplemented with questions more directly related to the position being filled.

XII. Pastoral Candidate Reference List

This can be used either as a form or a check list to assure that the church obtains the names of persons who should be contacted in the process of reviewing any pastoral candidate. This will help assure that the references obtained include a cross section of persons, and certain key people who need to be contacted.

XIII. Pastoral Candidate Reference Release Form

This is a general release for the church to obtain information from the references provided on the form above and in other contexts.

XIV.   Pastoral Candidate Reference Check

This form is specifically designed to pursue the references for pastoral candidates. It includes very direct questions regarding issues of character, reputation and background.

XV.   Employment Check List

A general check list at the conclusion of the process to assure that all the bases have been covered.

GENERAL APPLICATION

Directions: All applicants should complete this General Application. Additional forms may be attached seeking information specifically related to the position for which you are applying.

General Information

Name _____

Address _____

Phone _____

Social security number _____

How long have you lived at your present address? _____

What was your prior address and how long did you live there?

_____

Are you of a minimum legal age to work? _____ yes _____ no

What position are you applying for? _____

Are you looking for full, part-time, or temporary employment? _____

What days and hours are you available for work?

_____

_____

Have you ever been employed by us before? _____ yes _____ no

Have you ever applied with us before? _____ yes _____ no

        What position? _____

        When? _____

Are you being referred to us by a present or past employee of ours? _____ yes _____ no

        If, so, who_____

Prior Work History:

Are you presently employed? _____ yes _____ no

May we contact your present employer at this time? _____ yes _____ no

List all prior employers:

Dates	Employer	Title/Responsiblities	Name of Superviser

Please list start/end salaries for all positions during last five years.

_____

_____

_____

Were you eligible for re-hire at positions held during last ten years? _____ yes _____ no
   If not, explain why.

Why did you terminate your employment at each position held during last ten years?

Position	Reason for Leaving

How many days were you absent from work last year? _____

How many days were you late for work last year? _____

Have you ever volunteered for or been employed by a church? ____ yes ____ no
      If so, note church and positions you held and dates:

_____

_____

_____

Have you ever been disciplined by a professional body or state agency
(such as by having a license suspended or revoked.)? ____ yes ____ no
      If so, explain circumstances

_____

_____

Criminal Record:

-Have you ever been convicted of a crime other than a minor traffic offense? ____ yes ____ no
      If so, please explain.

_____

_____

Are you currently involved in any legal proceedings? ____ yes ____ no
      If so, please explain.

_____

_____

Military:

Were you ever in the military? ____ yes ____ no

    Dates? _____

    What branch, rank? _____

    List major responsibilities _____

    _____

    Reason for discharge? Please explain._____ ___

Education:

	Name	City	Dates of Attendance	Degree/Diploma

High School: _____

College(s)   _____

             _____

Other Education _____

Special awards, recognition, training, honors

    _____

    _____

Personal:

Please describe any additional skills, training, or experience that you feel would better prepare you for this position within our organization.

    _____

    _____

    _____

    _____

    _____

Please describe any personal characteristics that you feel better prepare you for this position within our organization.

_____

_____

_____

_____

The next two questions may be answered during your interview if you prefer. Your answer will NOT automatically disqualify you from employment with us.

Have you ever been a victim of child abuse? ____ yes ____ no

Have you ever been a victim of sexual abuse? ____ yes ____ no

References

Business References (Provide name, company/position, phone, address)

1. _____

_____

2. _____

_____

3. _____

_____

Personal References (Provide name, phone, address)

1. _____

_____

2. _____

_____

3. _____

_____

Christian Commitments:

Please attach to this application a statement of your Christian faith and experience. (Conversion, spiritual growth, etc.)

Of what church are you a member?

_____

Describe your current involvement with your church. (e.g. Activities in which participate.)

_____

_____

_____

What church leadership roles have you held?

_____

_____

What do you believe are the gifts and abilities which God has given you?

_____

_____

Have you read the church's Statement of Faith, and do you affirm it personally?
_____ yes _____ no

Have you read the Church Covenant, and will you conform your conduct to it?
_____ yes _____ no

Terms of Employment:

I understand that this church is an "at-will" employer and employment may be terminated at any time with or without cause. No information distributed or representations made by any representative of this church should be construed as an attempt to alter the "at-will" status of this position unless a contract is entered which specifically addresses and replaces its "at-will" employment status.

_____	_____
Applicant Signature	Date

Authorization and Reference Release:

The above information in this application is true and accurate to the best of my knowledge. I understand that false information will be grounds for termination.

I hereby authorize you to verify all information contained on this application with former employers, references, or appropriate personnel or resources. I further authorize that any personnel at the above listed places of employment or reference may disclose any and all information regarding my work history, personal characteristics, salary, work habits, or other areas of importance to this organization.

Furthermore, I waive the right to sue the aforementioned references for releasing such requested information.

I understand this authorization and termination policy and agree to the release and verification of the aforementioned information.

_____	_____
Applicant signature	Date

SAMPLE HANDBOOK DISCLOSURE FORM

I have read and understand the contents of this employee handbook. I understand that the employee handbook is an expression of current policy and may be altered at any time at the sole discretion of my employer. I further understand that no statements or implications contained in the employee handbook will be read to constitute an extension of my employment contract, and will in no way affect the status of my at-will employment."

_____   _____
Employee's Signature   Date

DECLARATION OF "AT-WILL" STATUS OF EMPLOYEE

This church is an "at-will" employer, and employment may be terminated at any time with or without cause. No information distributed or representations made by any representative of this church should be construed as an attempt to alter the "at-will" status of this position unless a contract is entered which specifically addresses and replaces its "at-will" employment status.

_____   _____
Applicant's signature   Date

INTERVIEW FORM

Applicant Name:

Position Interviewed For:

Interviewer:

Date:

I. Questions/Concerns From the Application (Address Further):

A. _____

   Response:

   _____

   _____

   _____

   _____

B. _____

   Response:

   _____

   _____

   _____

   _____

C. _____

   Response:

   _____

   _____

   _____

   _____

D. _____

    Response:

    _____

    _____

    _____

    _____

II. Ability to Perform the Essential Job Functions:

    Job Description has been reviewed with applicant: Yes ___ No ___

    Is there any reason why you would be unable to perform the specific function of the job as listed in the job description? Yes _____ No _____

    If so, which functions? _____

    What could we do as an employer to accommodate you, allowing you to perform adequately in this position?

    _____

    _____

    _____

III. Personal Characteristics: (There is no right or wrong answer. Answers only indicate which positions an applicant may be better suited for.)

    Are you most productive when working on group projects and in positions which require frequent interaction with others, or by yourself?

    _____

    _____

    Do you enjoy working on tasks alone? Why or why not?

    _____

    _____

    What prior positions have you particularly enjoyed? Why?

    _____

    _____

When considering prior positions you have held, what particular tasks did you enjoy the most?

_____

_____

Which of your prior positions have you enjoyed the least? Why?

_____

_____

Which tasks or duties have you enjoyed the least in prior positions?

_____

_____

What type of work environment do you prefer? (professional vs. casual; busy, lots of people vs. quiet, etc.)

_____

_____

How do you react to stressful situations?

_____

_____

Please describe one work situation/problem in which you were involved, including how you handled the situation.

_____

_____

_____

_____

How well do you feel you handle personnel problems?

_____

_____

_____

_____

Describe one personnel conflict you have encountered and how you were able to resolve it.

_____

_____

_____

_____

Are you more comfortable in a position in which a supervisor is usually available to answer questions or resolve problems?

_____

_____

_____

_____

How comfortable are you having to resolve a problem on your own, maybe even in an area you know little about?

_____

_____

_____

_____

Please describe a problem (any type) that you have encountered during your career. How was the problem resolved?

_____

_____

_____

_____

What have you learned from prior work experiences (either in solving problems, dealing with personnel issues, or other areas) that you feel might benefit you in this position?

_____

_____

_____

_____

IV. *Skills:*

How were you able to improve your skills or qualifications in your prior positions to your satisfaction?

_____

_____

_____

_____

What types of training did you receive in your prior positions which might be applicable to this position?

_____

_____

_____

_____

What type of training would you like to receive which might improve your skills, should you be selected for this position?

_____

_____

_____

_____

What do you feel are your strongest skills as they pertain to this position?

_____

_____

_____

_____

What do you feel are your weakest skills as they pertain to this position?

_____

_____

_____

_____

Should you be hired, what type of training could we offer you which might enhance your ability to perform in this position?

_____

_____

_____

_____

V. Goals and Aspirations:

Do you feel this position will be a positive move in your career progression? In what way?

_____

_____

_____

_____

Why do you want this position?

_____

_____

_____

_____

What do you see in the next step of your career progression after this position, should you be hired? In what time-frame?

_____

_____

_____

_____

What is your ultimate career goal and how do you plan to achieve it?

_____

_____

_____

_____

VI. *Additional Applicant Comments:*

Are there any additional comments you would like to make, even in areas I have not addressed, which might be important in this hiring decision?

_____

_____

_____

_____

VII. *Final Evaluation: (to be filled out once interview has ended)*

Note here comments on personal characteristics you observed during the interview which might impact his/her ability to perform in this position? (Appropriate attire, communication skills, sociability, poise, motivation, level of interest in the position, motivation to advance, ability to work alone/with others, etc.)

_____

_____

_____

_____

Note comments on this individual's skills which might impact his/her ability to perform in this position? (Indicate need for further training, good technical skills, willing to learn or train, particular training in specific areas, etc.)

_____

_____

_____

_____

Any outstanding characteristics observed?

_____

_____

_____

Any particular weaknesses observed?

_____

_____

_____

Any areas which require further attention, follow-up, or verification before considering this person any further?

_____

_____

_____

_____

Any questions that raise a doubt as to the proper "fit" of this person for this position? (Consider task oriented/people oriented; needs supervision/able to solve problems on own; team player and able to work with others/able to work alone; is a good/poor problem solver; would seek further training as position demands; would be happy in a "dead-end" position/would be seeking promotion to supervisory position one day, etc.)

_____

_____

_____

_____

_____

_____

_____

_____

_____

_____

_____   _____
Interviewer's signature   Date

CHILD-CARE INTERVIEW SUPPLEMENT

Applicant Name: _____

Position Interviewed For: _____

Interviewer: _____

Date: _____

I. *Statistics:*

Are you sixteen years of age or older?   yes _____   no _____

Are you at least twenty one years old if you are applying for a supervisory or director position?   yes _____   no _____

If applying for a supervisory or director position, are you literate?   yes ____   no ____

II. *Experience:*

What experience have you had working with children?

_____

_____   _____

_____

What ages were the children you've worked with?

_____

_____

What did you like best about it?

_____

_____

_____

What did you like least about it?

_____

_____

_____

How many children did you work with at once?

_____

Were you comfortable with this workload? Please explain.

_____

_____

_____

What number would you be most comfortable supervising?

_____

_____

What age group are you least comfortable working with? Why?

_____

_____

_____

What would make you more comfortable working with this age group?

_____

_____

Do you feel more comfortable working in a calm environment?

_____

_____

How do you feel about working in a hectic environment?

_____

_____

_____

Do you tend to lose patience when work is chaotic?

_____

_____

_____

III. *Training:*

What formal training, if any, have you had which would relate to this position? When?

_____

_____

_____

What informal training, if any, have you had which would relate to this position? When?

_____

_____

_____

What additional training could we offer you that would better prepare you for this position?

_____

_____

_____

What additional training could we offer you that would increase your job related skills?

_____

_____

Would you be willing to take advantage of such training?

_____

_____

_____

IV. Personal Background:

Please describe the relationship amongst your family members as you were growing up.

_____

_____

_____

_____

_____

What type of disciplinary measures were utilized?

_____

_____

_____

What type of discipline do you feel is most effective?

_____

_____

_____

Have you ever been physically or sexually abused?

_____

_____

_____

V. Interviewer's comments (complete after interview is concluded):

_____

_____

_____

_____

_____

_____

_____

_____

_____

_____   _____
Interviewer's signature   Date

VOLUNTEER NURSERY WORKER REGISTRATION FORM

As a volunteer nursery worker, please complete the following form which will assist our church's nursery care program in providing quality child care.

Name   _____

Maiden name   _____

Address   _____

               _____

Phone (H) _____

Last Previous Residence:

Address   _____

               _____

How long have you been attending this church? _____

How long have you been a member of this church? _____

Previous church affiliations (name, city). _____

Have you ever been employed in a non-church nursery, or any child care or elementary school context?   ___Yes ___ No   If "yes" please note below where and when.

    Where   Employee or Volunteer   Dates _____

_____

_____

(Add additional pages if necessary.)

Have you raised infant and pre-school children in your home (your own or others)?
    ____Yes ____No

Have you been a volunteer in a church nursery before?
    ____Yes ____No If yes, note where and when

_____

_____

Please note any formal education you have received in child care.

_____

_____

_____

Note any certificates or licenses you have which may reflect on your skills and abilities in working with infants and pre-school children?

_____

_____

_____

Have you ever been charged with or convicted of child abuse or child neglect?

_____Yes _____No

Have you been a victim of child abuse or neglect?

_____Yes _____No

Have you ever been denied legal custody of your children in any legal proceeding, including divorce decrees or settlements?

_____Yes _____No   Is so, please explain circumstances.

_____

_____

_____

What special skills or gifts do you have which will help you be an effective nursery volunteer?

_____

_____

_____

Note any special training or experience:

First Aid _____

Assisting children with handicaps _____

Other _____

What health factors may affect your ability to function as a volunteer, or impact the children? (e.g. communicable diseases, limitations on your physical abilities.)

_____

_____

_____

Provide the following information on your medical insurance and physician.

Current medical insurer: _____

Policy Number: _____

Family physician:

Name _____

Address _____

Phone _____

Are your willing to participate in volunteer nursery staff team meetings and training programs?
_____Yes _____No

Have you read the church's policy statements regarding nursery workers, and do you agree to abide by these guidelines?
_____Yes _____No

_____
Sign above   Date

VOLUNTEER DRIVER REGISTRATION FORM

We deeply appreciate your willingness to assist the church in driving your own or the church's vehicles to enable our ministry. Please complete the following form which will assist our church and assure appropriate insurance coverage and handing of emergencies.

Name _____

Maiden name _____

Address _____

_____

Phone (H) _____ (W) _____

Spouse: Name _____

Address (if different) _____

Phone _____

Closest Relative: Name _____

Address _____

_____

Phone _____

Last Previous Residence:

Address _____

_____

How long have you been attending this church? _____

How long have you been a member of this church? _____

Previous church affiliation (name, city). _____

Driver's License Information:

Name on license? _____

Type? _____

Any restrictions? _____

Expiration date? _____

In what other states have you had a driver's license in the last ten years?

_____

_____

Have you had any moving traffic violation arrests or convictions in the last five years?
(Include speeding, reckless driving, DUI, no operator's license and any other violations
other than parking tickets, expired inspection stickers and similar minor non-moving
violations

_____Yes ____No   If so, please note the violation and date

Charge   Conviction (Yes/No/Reduced)   Date   Place _____

_____

_____

_____

_____

Have you been denied a driver's license, or had it revoked or suspended?
_____Yes ____No   If so, please note the date and circumstances.

Provide the following insurance information.

Current insurance company: _____

Policy Number: _____

Agents name: _____

Agent's Address: _____

Agent's Phone Number: _____

How long have you been insured by them? _____

What is the extent of liability coverage? _____

Provide the following information on your medical insurance and physician.

Current medical insurer: _____

Policy Number: _____

Family physician:

Name _____

Address _____

Phone _____

Have you ever had a job which involved substantial driving (e.g. school bus, delivery work, long haul trucking, traveling sales position.)
_____Yes ____No If so, please note the date and circumstances.

_____

_____

Have you driven any of the following to the extent that you feel comfortable and competent? (Ck below)

_____ Automatic shift automobile
_____ Manual shift automobile
_____ Small van
_____ Pick-up truck
_____ School type bus
_____ Motor home
_____ Care-trailer combination
_____ Large truck

Have you read, understood, and do you agree to abide by, the Volunteer Driver Church Policy statement? (answer and sign below)

_____ Yes _____ No

Do you agree to advise the church immediately of any of the following: (answer and sign below) ___Yes ___ No

A change in insurance coverage (amount, company, or agency)
Moving violations
Revocation, suspension or any other change in driver's license

_____
Sign above   Date

WORK PROJECTS/MISSION TRIP
VOLUNTEER INFORMATION FORM

Project Name/Activity: _____

Name _____

Address _____

_____

Phone (H) _____(W)_____

Spouse: Name _____

Address (if different) _____

Phone (H) _____(W)_____

Closest Relative: Name _____

Address _____

_____

Phone (H)_____

Last Previous Residence:

Address _____

_____

How long have you been attending this church? _____

How long have you been a member of this church? _____

Previous church affiliation (name, city). _____

Family physician:

Name _____

Address _____

Phone _____

1. Have you been informed about the purposes, activities, locations and any special risks associated with this mission trip/work project?

____Yes   ____No

2. Have you been advised of the housing accommodations, arrangements for meals, and travel arrangements for this project?

       ____Yes   ____No

3. Do you have any physical limitations which may affect your ability to participate in all or some of these activities or which will require some special accommodations? (e.g. heavy lifting, working at heights, strenuous activities, work at high altitudes.)

_____

_____

_____

4. Please note which of the special skills noted below you possess and in the blanks note others which you may possess that will be of relevance to this project.

Skill	None	Little	Average	Experienced
General Carpentry				
Home Construction				
Cabinet Work				
Masonry				
Painting				
Decorating				
Cleaning				
Furniture Finishing				
Demotion of buildings				
Cement/Concrete				
Plumbing/Water Supply				
Agricultural Work				
English as Second Language				
Cooking/Food Service				
Nursing				
Medical Technician				
Dental Assistant				
Physician				
Dentist				

With which of the following tools are you comfortable and experienced?

Tool/Item	Some Skill	Considerable Experience
Chain saw		
Table saw		
Tractor		
Handsaws		
Drills		
Cement mixer		
Paint sprayers		
Air driven tools		
Ax		
Hoe		
Shovel		
Hammers		
Cookstoves		

Note languages in which you have conversational or greater proficiency.

_____

_____

Note any special medical or dietary needs.

_____

_____

Please check and add comments on training/skills related to health and rescue skills?

___ Lifesaving Certificate
___ First Aid training
___ EMT training
___ Practical Nursing
___ Physician's Assistant
___ Doctor (note practice areas)
___ Nurse
___ Dentist
___ Dental Hygienist
___ Dental Assistant
___ Veterinary Medicine
___ Physical Therapist
___ Medical Technician (note type)
___ Pharmacist
___ Optometry
___ Audiologist

Comments on Skills: _____

_____

If this project involves overseas activities, complete this section:

Do you have a current passport?   Number_____ Exp. Date _____

Have you received information on recommended vaccinations?

___ Yes ___ No

List current vaccinations?

_____

_____

_____

In what countries have you previously traveled?

_____

_____

_____

Have you been involved in work or mission projects overseas before. ___ Yes ___No
If so, please note place and nature of activities.

_____

_____

Have you confirm that you medical insurance will provide protection overseas?

_____ Yes _____ No

Preferred Work Patterns

_____ Am willing to be a team leader
_____ Prefer to be a team member, but not a leader
_____ Prefer to work on my own

VOLUNTEERS WITH CHILDREN AND YOUTH GROUPS: INFORMATION FORM

Name _____

Address _____

_____

Phone (H) _____(W)_____

Spouse: Name _____

Address (if different) _____

Phone (H) _____(W)_____

Closest Relative: Name _____

Address _____

_____

Phone (H)_____

Last Previous Residence:

Address _____

_____

How long have you been attending this church? _____

How long have you been a member of this church? _____

Previous church affiliation (name, city). _____

Family physician:

Name _____

Address _____

Phone _____

Last Two Previous Residences:

1. Dates of Residence _____

Address _____

_____
       city   county   state

2. Dates of Residence _____

    Address   _____

           _____
           city   county   state

How long have you been attending this church? _____

How long have you been a member of this church? _____

Previous church affiliations (name, city). _____

Have you ever been worked in a public or private school context? ___Yes ___ No
If "yes" please note below where and when.

      Where_____ Employee or Volunteer_____ Dates_____

      _____

      _____

      (Add additional pages if necessary.)

Were you involved as a youth in any church or other youth groups (e.g. scouts, YWAM, Acteens, etc. If so, note the groups and ages of your participation.

      _____

      _____

Have you raised school children in your home (your own or others)?
      ____Yes ____No

Have you been a volunteer in a church youth or children's ministries before?
      ____Yes ____No If yes, note where and when.

      _____

      _____

Please note any formal education you have received in youth work or ministry.

_____

_____

_____

Note any certificates or licenses you have which may reflect on your skills and abilities in working with youth?

_____

_____

_____

Have you ever been charged with or convicted of child abuse or child neglect?

_____Yes _____No

Have you been a victim of child abuse or neglect?

_____Yes _____No

Have you ever been denied legal custody of your children in any legal proceeding, including divorce decrees or settlements?

_____Yes _____No   Is so, please explain circumstances.

_____

_____

_____

Have you ever been convicted of a felony? If so, note offense, date and sentence.

_____

_____

What special skills or gifts do you have which will help you be an effective youth volunteer?

_____

_____

_____

Which of the following are areas of special interest and ability?

_____ Leading youth Bible studies
_____ Leading youth recreational activities
_____ Overnight camping-type activities
_____ Back-yard Bible clubs
_____ Community service activities
_____ General supervision - chaperone
_____ Canoeing
_____ Hiking - backpacking
_____ Biking
_____ Work projects
_____ Overnight lock-ins
_____ Leading discussion groups
_____ Mountain climbing
_____ Missions education
_____ Sunday School teaching

Note any special training or experience:

First Aid _____

Assisting youth with handicaps _____

Other _____

What health factors may affect your ability to function as a volunteer, or impact the children? (e.g. communicable diseases, limitations on your physical abilities.)

_____

_____

_____

Provide the following information on your medical insurance and physician.

        Current medical insurer: _____

        Policy Number: _____

        Family physician:

                Name _____

                Address _____

                Phone _____

Have you read the church's policy statements regarding youth ministry and activities, and do you agree to abide by these guidelines?

        ____Yes   ____No

                            _____

                                Sign above   Date

REFERENCE RELEASE FORM

Reference:

_____
Company (if applicable)

_____
Address

_____
Phone

_____ ext. _____
Contact

_____ ext. _____
Contact

_____ ext. _____
Contact

_____ ext. _____
Contact

I hereby authorize <u>(church name, City, State),</u> to verify all information contained on this application with former employers, references, or appropriate personnel or resources. I further authorize that any personnel at the listed places of employment or reference may disclose any and all information regarding my work history, personal characteristics, salary, work habits, or other areas of importance to this organization. (Each employer should further customize this list.)

Furthermore, I waive the right to sue the aforementioned references for releasing such requested information.

I understand this authorization and termination policy and agree to the release and verification of the aforementioned information.

_____   _____
Applicant's signature   Date

REFERENCE CHECK FORM

Applicant's Name: _____

Position Applied For: _____

Name of Reference: _____

Company: _____

Address: _____

Phone: _____

Person Conducting Reference Check: _____

Date: _____

Reference Release Form Sent to Reference? yes _____ no _____

I. *Application Verification Questions: (Place a check mark beside those questions that are verified by the reference. If a reference's response differs from the application, note the reference's response in the lined areas.)*

What was the employee's title?

_____

Reference Check Form, p. 2

What were his/her major responsibilities?

_____

_____

_____

_____

Were you his/her immediate supervisor? Who was?

_____

_____

What were his/her starting and ending date?

_____

What were his/her starting and ending salary?

_____

Is he/she eligible for re-hire?

_____

For what reason did he/she leave your employment?

_____

_____

How many absences did he/she have last year?

_____

How many days was he/she tardy?

_____

*II. Applicant's Fitness for this Position: (Utilize the Job Description as well as the
Statement of Faith, Statement of Moral Obligation, or Church Rules and
Policies where appropriate.)*

Does the applicant have the skills required by this position?

_____

_____

In your estimation, does this applicant have the personality and disposition required
of this position?

_____

_____

Would you feel comfortable placing this applicant in this position?

_____

_____

Are there any reasons why you might hesitate to place the applicant in this position, were you the one doing the hiring for it?

_____

_____

Without listing particular details, do you feel we should continue our search for a more suitable applicant for this position?

_____

_____

Additional questions pertaining to this particular position: (These questions should be formulated before the reference is called.)

1. _____

_____

2. _____

_____

3. _____

_____

4. _____

_____

III. *Personal characteristics:*

How well did this person relate to and work with others?

_____

_____

_____

_____

Did you enjoy working with this individual?

_____

_____

_____

_____

What were this applicant's greatest assets?

_____

_____

_____

_____

What were this applicant's greatest weaknesses?

_____

_____

_____

_____

Are there any additional comments you could make that might be helpful to us?

_____

_____

_____

IV. Secondary references: (List the names suggested by the reference as others who might be able to offer a reference.)

1. Name _____

    Address _____

    Phone _____

2. Name _____

    Address _____

    Phone _____

3. Name _____

    Address _____

    Phone _____

_____

Person Conducting Reference Check's Signature

_____

Title

_____

Date

PASTORAL CANDIDATE REFERENCE LIST

Please list the following references, and sign the attached Release Form authorizing contact with such persons and your waiver of any rights of confidentiality regarding information they may have related to your fitness for ministry.

I. Churches

(List all churches you have served, the dates of your service, and the chairmen of the Deacons during your service.)

Church	Location	Dates of Service	Chairmen of Deacons

II. Please provide the name and current address of the Director of Missions in the area of your last three places of ministry

_____

_____

_____

III. Name of three pastoral colleagues in your last place of ministry -- include address and phone number.

_____

_____

_____

IV. Name of two academic references, at least one from seminary and, if applicable, at least one from any post-M.Div. graduate work

_____

_____

V. Name of Bank and officer of bank in last two places of ministry

_____

_____

VI. Name, address and phone of four lay persons with whom you are not related who are familiar with your philosophy and practice of ministry.

_____

_____

_____

_____

PASTORAL CANDIDATE REFERENCE RELEASE FORM

I hereby authorize <u>(Church, City, State)</u> to verify all information contained in my application or other written communications, including all former churches in which I have served as a pastor, been a member or been ordained. I recognize that this verification process will include contacts with church officers, members, pastoral collagues, Association and State Convention personnel, as well as other business and professional references. I further authorize that any personnel at places of employment, churches or references may disclose any and all information regarding my work history, personal characteristics, salary, work habits, or other areas of importance to this organization.

Furthermore, I waive the right to sue the aforementioned churches, their members and officers, or references for releasing such requested information.

I understand this authorization and termination policy and agree to the release and verification of the aforementioned information.

_____   _____
Applicant's signature   Date

PASTORAL CANDIDATE REFERENCE CHECK

Candidate Name: _____

Reference Name: _____

Reference Phone: _____

Interviewer(s): _____

Date: _____

How long have you known the candidate? _____

In what capacity have you known the candidate? (Member/officer in church he pastors; professional colleague in ministry; co-ministry role in church; business associate; etc.)

_____

_____

Are you aware that he is a potential candidate for pastor of our church? _____

Are you aware of the major reasons he might be open to a new call?

_____

_____

Do you have any information which would give you any reservations about this candidate's appropriateness for pastoral ministry?

_____

_____

Are you aware of any disciplinary proceedings involving charges against this candidate by his ordaining church, any other church body, or other professional agency or body?

_____

_____

Have you had any personal experience or heard reports from others who have questioned this candidate's integrity, honesty, ethics or conduct?

_____

_____

Do you know if this person has ever left a job or ministry position because of charges or accusations related to his conduct or beliefs?   What do you know of the circumstances?

_____

_____

Would you positively recommend this person for ministry at our church?   Why?

_____

_____

Have you had any reports of sexual misconduct? What were those reports?

_____

_____

Have any questions been raised regarding his personal finances or his handling of church funds?

_____

_____

What is his reputation among his professional colleagues?

_____

_____

Based on your knowledge and his reputation, is his marriage healthy and stable?

_____

_____

Do you know of any conduct of the candidate's family members which would raise any serious questions about our church's consideration of him for a ministry here?

_____

_____

Do you have any confidential information you are not free to reveal to us concerning his fitness for ministry?

yes_____   no_____

Can you provide the name(s) of other persons who worked closely with the candidate or otherwise are well acquainted who would be helpful reference to our church in assessing the candidate?

_____

_____

EMPLOYMENT CHECKLIST

_____ Application completed

_____ I-9 completed

_____ I-9 filed in separate "I-9 notebook"

_____ Reference check forms completed

_____ Driver's record check form completed

_____ Criminal record check form completed

_____ Statement of faith presented; signed by applicant; returned to folder

_____ Statement of moral obligations presented; signed by applicant; returned to folder

_____ Church rules and policies presented; signed by applicant; returned to folder

_____ Interview conducted:

Date: _____

Interviewer: _____

_____ Job description presented and signed (N/A if applicant was not being interviewed for a specific position)

_____ Copies of signed reference release forms made before being sent; filed back in employment packet

_____ References contacted; forms completed; filed

_____ Criminal record checked

_____ Driver's record checked

_____ Rejection letter sent; copy filed

_____ Acceptance letter sent; copy filed

II. Sample Church By-Law Provisions

A. PERSONNEL COMMITTEE

B. PASTOR-SEARCH COMMITTEE

C. SELECTION AND CALL OF PASTOR

D. INTERIM LEADERSHIP

E. TERMINATION OF PASTOR

F. EMPLOYMENT AGREEMENTS

G. NON-PASTOR STAFF SELECTION PROCESS

H. DAY CARE: PUBLIC STATEMENT OF CHRISTIAN COMMITMENT AND HIRING POLICY

SAMPLE CHURCH BY-LAW PROVISIONS ON EMPLOYMENT MATTERS INCLUDING STAFF SELECTION PROCESS

NOTE: These clauses are not intended to be "models" or even preferred options, but are illustrative of the sort of provisions which should be included in church bylaws or other governing documents. Local church practice in such areas as selection of the Pastor-Search Committee vary widely, and church documents should reflect the local practice.

A. Personnel Committee

The committee shall be composed on (number) members, elected to rotating terms of three years with one-third of the members being elected each year. The Committee shall have the following responsibilities:

1. In consultation with the pastor, to evaluate the non-ministerial staff needs of the church and make recommendations to the church regarding such positions.

2. After a thorough evaluation process, to recommend to the church persons to fill non-ministerial staff positions.

3. When circumstances warrant to suspend or dismiss non-ministerial staff.

4. To prepare job descriptions for all employees which shall include the employees' responsibilities and indicate to whom the employee shall report.

5. To annually review the performance, needs and concerns of employees, and to recommend salaries and benefits, and to make such other recommendations to the employee(s), pastor or church as they may deem appropriate to further the effective work of the staff.

6. To maintain the personnel files in a manner consistent with law and appropriate confidentility.

B. Pastor Search Committee

On the Sunday following the announcement of the resignation of the Pastor or as soon thereafter as practically possible, the members of the church shall be invited to submit to the deacons their recommendations for persons to serve on the Pastor Search Committee. From those recommendations, the deacons shall nominate and present to the church a proposed committee of seven members who are willing to serve, and who are representative of the various programs and ministries of the church. At that time, other nominations shall be accepted from the floor. A ballot shall be composed listing all nominees who are willing to serve and shall be submitted on the Sunday following the nominations to the church membership, for the election of the members of the Pastor Search Committee. Each church member may vote for up to seven nominees, and the seven persons receiving the greatest number of votes shall compose the Pastor Search Committee. The Committee shall select its own officers. All related and proper expenses incurred by the committee in its search for a Pastor shall be borne by the church. After the call of a new Pastor, the committee will continue to serve as a liaison between the Pastor and the church for a period of at least three months following the Pastor's commencing work with the church. In the event of a vacancy on the Pastor Search Committee, the procedure outlined above shall be repeated with the deacons nominating a replacement, nominations being accepted from the floor, and voting by the church membership on the person to fill the vacancy.

C. Selection and Call of Pastor

In the event of a vacancy in the office of Pastor, the Pastor Search Committee shall seek out and recommend to the church a person whose Christian character and qualifications have been carefully examined and are found to fit the person for the office of Pastor. Any person considered for the office shall be a Baptist in good standing and in friendly harmony with the convention programs with which the church is affiliated. This Committee's recommendation will constitute a nomination, and no nominations shall be made except by the Committee. The Committee shall bring only one nomination at a time to the church for consideration, and no candidate shall be invited to preach for the church prior to his formal nomination. The Committee shall establish a process by which the church may become acquainted with the candidate. The formal call of the Pastor shall take place at a business meeting especially set for that purpose and for which at least one week's notice has been given to the membership. The vote on the extension of a call shall be by secret ballot and an affirmative vote of three-fourths of the members present and voting shall be required for a call. If the Committee's recommendation fails to receive the required vote, the meeting shall be adjourned without debate, and the Committee will then seek out another candidate to recommend to the church.

D. Interim Leadership

On the Sunday following the announcement of the resignation of the Pastor or as soon thereafter as is practical, the deacons shall nominate to the church membership for its approval a committee of three to serve as the Interim Leadership Committee. This committee will be charged with the responsibility of:

(1) Recommending an Interim Pastor to the church, or, if they deem advisable, finding persons to fill the pulpit on a week-by-week basis.
(2) Recommending to the church the compensation of the Interim Pastor or pulpit supplies.
(3) Overseeing the general operation of the church, its staff, and programs during the interim period.

This committee shall serve until the installation of a new Pastor. Members of the Interim Leadership Committee shall not be eligible to be on the Pastor Search Committee.

E. Termination of Pastor

The Pastor shall serve under a continuing call until the pastoral relationship is dissolved at the request of the Pastor or the church.

(a) Resignation: The Pastor may resign but shall normally provide four weeks notice before the termination of his services. By agreement with the deacons, such a resignation may be effective with lesser notice.
(b) Removal: A Pastor may be removed by a majority vote of the members present and voting at a properly called meeting.

(1) The officers and the members shall make every effort to follow biblical principles including the processes set forth in Matthew 18 in dealing with conflicts regarding pastoral staff. Every effort should be extended to permit reconciliation of conflicts in a manner consistent with our Christian faith and doctrine.

(2) Any vote on the removal of the Pastor is subject to the following conditions and procedures:

(a) A congregational meeting and vote on the removal shall be called only where a majority of the deacons have adopted a resolution calling for such, or upon written demand for such a vote signed by not less than twenty church members, and presented to the deacons or a business session.

(b) The time and date of the meeting shall be set no later than forty days after the deacons have voted for such a congregational decision, or the written demand from members has been received.

(c) The Pastor must be given an opportunity to be heard at the church meeting prior to the vote.

(3) Removal shall be effective immediately upon the adoption of a motion terminating the Pastor, but salary and benefits shall continue for not less than thirty days. Any resolution to dismiss may also contain recommendations concerning other financial aspects of the termination including severance pay.

F. Employment Agreements

The church by congregational action may enter into a formal employment agreement with the Pastor which sets forth the compensation package, vacation policies and other matters related to the office of Pastor except that no such agreement may create a binding employment contract which limits the exclusive rights of the membership of the church to terminate at any time the Pastor's employment and any financial obligations related to that employment.

G. Non-Pastor Staff Selection Process

Section A: General Practice

The church may employ such staff as it deems appropriate to fulfill its mission. In the cases of all staff, the congregation shall approve job descriptions which shall be set forth in the Policies and Procedures Manual. General personnel policies, as appropriate, shall also be proposed by appropriate committees and, if adopted by the church, included in the Policies and Procedures Manual.

Section B. Ministerial Staff Other Than Senior Pastor.

The church may employ from time to time, as it deems in the best interest of the ministry and program of the church, other ministerial staff members who shall assist the Pastor in their specified areas of responsibility. Ministerial staff shall include associate pastors, ministers of youth, college students, music, evangelism, and any other staff positions involving spiritual, pastoral, educational or nurturing ministries of the church.

1. Selection. In the event of a vacancy among the other ministerial staff or if empowered by the church to employ a person to fill a new staff position, the personnel committee shall appoint, with the consent of the deacons and the approval of the church in business session, a Search Committee to recommend a person to fill the vacancy. The committee shall establish a process for identifying candidates, reviewing their credentials, assessing their spiritual maturity and gifts, and weighing their appropriateness for the specific ministry needs of the church. The Search Committee, after consultation with the Personnel and Finance Committees, and review of its recommendation by the deacons, shall present its recommendation to the church at any regular or called business meeting, provided that announcement of the nomination has been made from the pulpit on the Sunday prior to the business meeting or by written notice to the families of the church seven days before the business meeting. The committee shall provide to the church appropriate background information on the candidate and the basis of the committee's recommendation. A two-thirds vote of those members present and voting shall be necessary for the confirmation of the Search Committee's nominee.

2. Accountability. Ministerial staff shall report and be accountable to the Senior Pastor. The Pastor and personnel committee shall regularly review the work of each ministerial staff member, and annually evaluate and make recommendations to the staff member concerning his/her ministry.

3. Removal. Ministerial staff may be terminated by action of the congregation acting on recommendation of the Personnel Committee and deacons. Such recommendation may include proposals concerning any financial aspects associated with the dismissal such as severance pay.

4. Interim Staff. Interim ministerial staff may be employed for a period not to exceed six months. Proposed interim staff shall be recommended to the church by the Personnel Committee working in consultation with the Pastor, deacons and other appropriate committees. Such interim staff nominees shall be subject to approval by the church at a proper business meeting. Employed interim ministerial staff may be renewed beyond the six month term upon specific recommendation of the Personnel Committee and approval by the congregation.

Section C: Non-Ministerial Staff

The church may employ full or part time non-ministerial staff to assist in fulfilling the church's mission. Such positions would include, but not be limited to, clerical, bookkeeping and custodial services.

1. The Personnel Committee in consultation with the Pastor and appropriate committees shall develop and recommend to the church for adoption, job descriptions for any such positions.

2. The Personnel Committee in consultation with the finance committee shall make recommendations to the church for the funding of such positions.

3. The Personnel Committee in consultation with the Pastor shall establish processes for announcing available positions, and receiving applications. The committee shall make recommendations to the deacons of persons to fill non-

ministerial staff. With the deacon's concurrence, the Pastor may on behalf of the church proceed to employ the recommended persons.

4. The Personnel Committee shall regularly review the work of all non-ministerial staff, and shall annually review with each staff member their tasks and performance. The committee shall make such recommendations to the church or staff member as it deems appropriate.

5. In the event the Personnel Committee in consultation with the Pastor believes that the employment of any non-ministerial staff member should be terminated, the Personnel Committee shall make a recommendation to that effect to the deacons. The deacons may concur or in its discretion, forward the recommendation to the church council or the congregation. If the deacons concur or the body to whom they refer it concurs, then the Pastor shall dismiss the employee. The Personnel Committee shall include in its recommendation any financial proposals associated with dismissal such as severance pay.

6. Interim non-ministerial staff may be employed by action of the Personnel Committee provided the deacons are given an opportunity to respond to the proposed interim staff recommendation.

H. Day Care: Public Statement of Christian Commitment and Hiring Policy

The Day Care program is a ministry of _____ Baptist Church, and seeks in all respects to reflect the principles and faith of the church. Our love and care for children, and desire to see them grow and mature into the persons God intended them to be, is part of our Christian faith. Our Scriptures tell us of the openness of our Lord to children, and his delight in them. We want in all we do to model that love and delight in children. Our faith also affirms the crucial importance of parenting, and in all we do we will seek to be enablers and encouragers of the parents of the children entrusted to us.

As a church day care, you will note that our facilities and program include symbols and stories from our faith and heritage. We believe that effective day care includes appropriate age-related stories and activities that teach respect for persons, love of neighbor, love of God, and the development of all the gifts God has given to each child. While we will not impose any religious faith or belief on any child, and we will respect the religious commitments of the parents of the children in our care, we are open about our faith and traditions and they are evident in our music, symbols and stories as well as in the faith of our teachers. All the staff of the Church, including the staff of the Day Care, are selected not only with a view to their professional competencies, and commitments to their ministry, but also to their personal commitment to Christ and their discipleship.

III. Bibliography

American Baptist Churches. *Calling an American Baptist Minister and Church Reflections.* American Baptist Churches USA: Valley Forge, PA, 1991.

Bailey, Jack. Before You Make That Final Hiring Decision. *Church Administration: A Journal for Effectiveness in Ministry.* Vol. 34, #7, p. 20-21, 1992.

Bloss, Julie. *Employment Law: A Guide for Churches.* Church Management, Inc.: Austin, TX, 1993.

Center for the Study of Law and the Church, Samford University, "Gender Discrimination," *Law & Church.*, Summer, 1993.

Church Law & Tax Report. October 1991, "Church and Denominational Liability for the Sexual Misconduct of Clergy."

Church-State Resource Center. *Minister's Legal Desk Reference.* Church-State Resource Center, Campbell University: Buies Creek, NC, 1991.

Couser, Richard. *Ministry and the American Legal System: A Guide for Clergy, Lay Workers, and Congregations.* Fortress Press: Minneapolis, Minn. 1993.

Employment and Labor Relations Law Committee, Section on Litigation. *Employment Litigation.* American Bar Association: Chicago, Illinois 1994.

Frieze, Rex. I. *Administrative Forms Manual for Churches And Other Ministries.* Frieze and Company: Orlando, Florida 1993.

Gammon & Grange. A Prudent Volunteer Program for Nonprofits. *Nonprofit Alert.* NP9301-1, 1993.

Gammon & Grange. Avoiding Employment Discrimination in the Nonprofit Organization. *Nonprofit Alert.* NP9312-1, 1993.

Gammon & Grange. Basic Requirements Under The Americans with Disabilities Act. *Nonprofit Alert.* NP9109-3, 1993.

Gammon & Grange. Minimizing Liability by Updating Your Employment Application. *Nonprofit Alert.* NP9306-1, 1994.

Gammon & Grange. Minimizing Liability for Negligent Hiring and Supervision. *Nonprofit Alert.* NP9101-1, 1993.

Gammon & Grange. Nonprofit Employers and the Fair Labor Standards Act (FLSA). *Nonprofit Alert.* NP9208-1, 1993.

Gammon & Grange. The Right of Religious Employers to Select Employees Based on Religion. *Nonprofit Alert.* NP9103-1, 1993.

Grubbs, Bruce. *The Pastor Selection Committee.* The Sunday School Board of the Southern Baptist Convention: Nashville, Tenn. 1977.

Hammar, Richard R., *Pastor, Church and Law*, 2d ed. Christian Ministry Resources: Matthews, NC, 1991.

Hammar, Richard R., Klipowicz, Steven W. and Cobble, James F. Jr. *Reducing the Risk of Child Abuse in Your Church.*

Hendricks, Garland. *The Ongoing of a Baptist Church: The Ethics and Etiquette Of Calling A Pastor.* The B.C. Morris Academy for Christian Studies, Gardner-Webb College: Boiling Springs, NC, 1984.

Ketchum, Bunty. *So You're on the Search Committee.* The Alban Institute, Inc.: Washington, DC, 1985.

Lamb, Robert L. and Howell, Stan. *Workbook for Staff Minister Search Committees: A Guide for Seeking a Staff Minister.* Baptist State Convention of North Carolina: Cary, NC, 1991.

Lansing, Carl F. *Legal Handbook Defense.* Navpress Publishing Group: Colorado Springs, Colorado 1992.

Levicoff, Steve. *Christian Counseling and the Law.* The Moody Bible Institute of Chicago, Illinois 1991.

MacMillan, Pat. *Hiring Excellence: Six Steps to Making Good People Decisions.* Navpress Publishing Group: Colorado Springs, Colorado 1992.

McMenamin & Kradovec. *Clergy and Teacher Malpractice: Recognition and Prevention.* Jomac Publishing, Inc.: Portland, Oregon.

Pastor-Church Relations. *Workbook for Search Committees.* Baptist State Convention: Cary, NC.

Oswald, Roy. *Finding Leaders for Tomorrow's Churches: The Growing Crisis in Clergy Recruitment.* The Alban Institute, Inc.: Washington DC, 1993.

Oswald, Roy. *New Beginnings: A Pastorate Start Up Workbook.* The Alban Institute, Inc.: Washington DC, 1989.

Phillips, Wm. Bud. *Pastoral Transitions: From Endings to New Beginnings.* The Alban Institute, Inc.: Washington DC, 1988.

Skupsky, Donald. *Recordkeeping Requirements.* Information Requirements Clearinghouse: Denver, Colorado 1991.

Skupsky, Donald. *Records Retention Procedures: Your Guide to Determine How Long to Keep Your Records and How to Safely Destroy Them!* Information Requirements Clearinghouse: Denver, Colorado 1991.

Wilson, Marlene. *How to Mobilize Church Volunteers.* Augsburg Publishing House: Minneapolis, Minn. 1983.

Tapes:

Bergida, Mike. *Hiring for Effectiveness*. Christian Management Association: Diamond Bar, California.

Campanelli, Richard. *Personnel Policy Manuals & Employee Handbooks: Legal Guidelines*. Christian Management Association: Diamond Bar, CA.

Campanelli, Richard. *Volunteers, Liability and Risk Management*. Christian Management Association: Diamond Bar, California.

Kasper, Dennis. *Labor Law Update*. Christian Management Association: Diamond Bar, California.

Kasper, Dennis. Personnel Legal Issues. *The Management Series: Human Resource Management*. Christian Ministries Management Association: Diamond Bar, California.

Kline, Rhonda. Testing and Assessment. *The Management Series: Human Resource Management*. Christian Ministries Management Association: Diamond Bar, California.

Nash, Sylvia. Recruiting & Hiring: How to Get the Right Person for the Job. *The Management Series: Human Resource Management*. Christian Ministries Management Association: Diamond Bar, California.

Thompson, Robert R. *Avoiding Legal Liability For Churches, Clergy, and Volunteers*. Christian Management Association: Diamond Bar, California.

Fold

Place
Stamp
Here

John Edwards
J.W. Edwards Publishing
2500 South State Street
Ann Arbor, Michigan 48106

Fold

Title of Book:_____

We've tried to make this publication as useful, accurate, and readable as possible. Please take 5 minutes to tell us if we succeeded. Your comments and suggestions will help us improve our publications. Thank you!

1. How did you acquire this publication:

☐ by mail order   ☐ at a meeting/convention   ☐ as a gift

☐ by phone order   ☐ at a bookstore   ☐ don't know

☐ other: (describe) _____

Please rate this publication as follows:

	Excellent	Good	Fair	Poor	Not Applicable
Readability: Was the book easy to read and understand?	☐	☐	☐	☐	☐
Examples/Cases: Were they helpful, practical? Were there enough?	☐	☐	☐	☐	☐
Content: Did the book meet your expectations? Did it cover the subject adequately?	☐	☐	☐	☐	☐
Organization and clarity: Was the sequence of text logical? Was it easy to find what you wanted to know?	☐	☐	☐	☐	☐
Illustrations/forms/checklists: Were they clear and useful? Were there enough?	☐	☐	☐	☐	☐
Physical attractiveness: What did you think of the appearance of the publication (typesetting, printing, etc.)?	☐	☐	☐	☐	☐

How could this publication be improved? What else would you like to see in it?

_____

_____

_____

Do you have other comments or suggestions? _____

_____

_____

Name _____

Firm/Company _____

Address _____

City/State/Zip _____

Phone _____

We appreciate your time and help.